T0193417

CHECKMATE

THE GAME OF LIFE

WESSAM ELDEIN

authorHOUSE°

AuthorHouse™
1663 Liberty Drive
Bloomington, IN 47403
www.authorhouse.com
Phone: 1 (800) 839-8640

Published by AuthorHouse 08/27/2019

ISBN: 978-1-7283-2422-7 (sc)
ISBN: 978-1-7283-2421-0 (e)

Library of Congress Control Number: 2019912617

Print information available on the last page.

This book is printed on acid-free paper.

Contents

To my kids, Ali, Omr, and Yihya. You are the reason I wrote this book, and you are the revelation of this book. In our journey together, I thought I was teaching you how to face life, but it turned out you were teaching me how to enjoy it.

To my wife, Shaden. If time were to go back, I would propose again and again and again.

To my parents and my siblings. You are the reason I am what I am. Thank you for being the family everyone wishes for.

To everyone I met or will meet in this journey of life, whether friend or foe, whether you helped or hurt me. Thank you for everything I learned from you.

Last but not least, to you. Yes, you, my friend who is reading these words now. Thank you for giving me the chance to be a part of your precious life, as you are now also a part of mine. I hope you enjoy this book, because I enjoyed talking to you.

Introduction

LIFE. Those four letters create a magic word, the dream of all dreams, and the reason behind all our actions, thoughts, and feelings. Life is the grand reward, the ultimate goal, and the only way.

When you dream about anything like true love, money, success, or even a job, you don't really dream about these things. You actually dream about how to enrich your life with these things. You dream about the tools you believe you need to live a better life!

When you are doing a good deed, either you're seeking a better lifestyle for someone, or you want to feel better about yourself by helping society and by reflecting on your life. Or perhaps you are seeking heaven after life, which is another form of life. In all three scenarios, and even for other scenarios that I overlooked, your goal is life, whether yours or someone else's, whether here or in another form (e.g., afterlife).

You may say, "Wait a minute. This concept is so selfish. When I fall in true love, I am willing to do anything for the person I love, not for myself. I am willing to give my life to make the other person happy."

Exactly. First of all, we are talking about life in general as the grand reward, not my life or your life.

Second, you are willing to give your life to your true love because you can't find anything more valuable to give to her or him. You believe that sacrificing your life will be your last option to save her or his life, so you are giving up a life to save a life.

You can give up your job to save your life, or you can give up your money to save your life, but you can't give up your life for those things.

In some cases, you may refuse to give up your job or your money. You may prefer to lose your life for moral reasons because you can't stand your life without your morals. In these cases, you prefer to have a better afterlife than this current life. No matter your beliefs about the forms of afterlife, you are giving up a life for a better life.

All scenarios will take us to the same fact: life is the grand reward.

You may be thinking, "This is common sense, and everything we do is for seeking a better life. What is the point?" Either you are seeing what you've read so far is common sense, or you disagree with it to a certain extent. I would like you to read it one more time and then answer the following questions.

If life is the most valuable thing we have, and we try to save it as much as we can—or we sacrifice it to show true love, or to stand for morals or certain beliefs—then why we don't read and learn the manual of life? Why do we keep playing the demo version of the game of life?

We think we are playing the game of life, but we are playing only the demo version. Why don't we download the full version with the help file and start playing the real game?

You say, "Are you telling me that this book is the help file for the game of life?"

I wish there was a short answer to this question, like yes or no, but this book is not your guide to living your life because there is no such thing. No one can tell you how to live your life.

However, this book is a theory about how to see life from different perspectives. Think of it as prescription glasses to make the picture clearer. It is a point of view that I want to share with you, and I want to hear your opinion and your point of view.

These prescription glasses may or may not fit your vision, and they may or may not make you see the picture clearer. You will never know until you try it!

You may agree or disagree with parts of the book—or with the whole book—but by the end of reading it, you will find that it doesn't matter whether you agree or disagree with it. What really matters is reading it!

Confused? There are two reasons why I want you to read this book.

1. Quite simply, I want you to buy the book!

2. We all have differences, but even with our differences in shape, race, color, religion, and language, we still have similarities. We still share some characteristics, and we still share some common ground. If you didn't agree with the theory in the book, but you can find common ground between you and me or between you and other readers, then you get the point of this book. After reading the book, you will end up saying one of two things.

   - **Ah, that's why! Now I get it!** Then please send me your feedback and let me see your perspective.

   - **Hmm, I didn't get it.** Then please send me your feedback and let me learn your perspective!

Do we have a deal?

Back to my point. If life is a game, I would love to see it as a chess game. It's not just because the strategies we need to apply and the decisions we need to make every day are the same as what chess players are using in their games. It's also because of the structure of life and how similar it is to the structure of chess. In life, you can see people as pawns, knights, bishops, rooks, queens, or kings. But if we zoom in, we will see that people will change between most of these shapes.

A person facing different situations can swing between these shapes back and forth. One shape will always dominate one's personality, but even with that, one still has all these shapes inside, and every once in a while, one of the shapes will jump to the surface. The key here is to control when and where these shapes show their faces!

What are these shapes or characters in the game and in life? Let's have a brief introduction.

King: The highest rank on the game, but with limitation on movements: only one step in any direction front, back, left, right, or diagonally. There is only one king on each side in chess. For a lot of people, being a king is a life goal. A few people are born as kings. The whole chess game is about protecting the king. In the game of life, the king is not just a rank or royalty; it could be someone you love, and it could also be the beliefs that you stand for or your ultimate goal. In general, the king in the game of life is what you are willing to sacrifice everything you have for, even your life, to save it.

Queen: The most powerful character in the game can cross the whole chessboard in all directions. Like the king, there is only one queen on each side. The game is about protecting the king, but the queen is a very important character to help reach that goal. In life, the queen could be someone you blindly trust and can count on 100 percent, like a friend. Or it could be a powerful tool that you can use to reach your goal.

Rook: The rook is another powerful character in chess. I see it as the queen's sidekick. It is the only piece beside the queen that can cross the whole chessboard on a straight line front, back, left, or right. In chess, each side has two rooks. In the game of life, I see rooks as family, culture, religion, and morals.

Bishop: The other sidekick of the queen, the bishop is only piece besides the queen that can cross the whole chessboard diagonally. Like the rook, there are two bishops on each side. I see bishops in the game of life as education, knowledge, and experience.

Knight: The unpredictable character. Two knights are on each side. The knight can move in an L shape in any direction. It's a very powerful piece that can help the player control the game if the player knows how and when to use it. In the game of life, I see knights as skills, flexibility, acceptance, and diversity.

Pawn: This is us. This is me, this is you, and this is almost everyone. This is how we start—and how we may end. For a lot of people who know how to play chess, this is the lowest piece. In chess we get eight pawns on each side. Usually, they can only move forward one step at a time, but they attack diagonally. They don't have the privilege of going back. It's the same in life: we can't retreat and go back on most of our decisions. The good news is if the pawn can survive crossing the whole chessboard, it can reincarnate as any character, queen, rook, bishop, or knight. This privilege is only for the pawn!

Starting as a pawn is not that bad. Ending as a pawn is not that bad either. It is all about the journey between the start and the end!

As you can see, every piece has its strengths and weaknesses. Every piece can decide how the game will go. Before we go on, I need you to remember, and keep remembering, a very important concept. You are not any of these pieces—you are all of them. You are the player. You are the one who controls all the pieces, and you are only one of these pieces when you decide to use it!

Now that we've had a brief introduction about chess pieces and what they represent, let us continue our journey to explore the game of life! Another similarity between life and chess is how the game is going. We think that phases of life and the people we meet at these different phases are discrete, but the truth is they are all related. They are all part of the big game. Life is not just one game of chess—it is multiple games, and all these games together form the big chess game, your life's game!

Let me give you an example to clarify this point.

Finishing high school is a chess game that ends up with either winning the game (checkmate) or losing the game. But when we look to the big picture, to one's whole-life chess game, finishing high school is just one move in the big game. It could be a good move or a bad move, but it is just one move, and it is not the end of the game.

This high school move could make the chances of winning the game higher or lower. It may force us to change our playing strategy, but at the end, we can still win or lose—or shall we say, win or learn.

In this book, you will find discrete points that look like they have nothing in common. At the end, you will find all these points together form the main concept of the book. You will find a link between all these points— the same link between your different phases of life, the same link between all the moves in the chess game from the beginning until "Checkmate."

That was the introduction ... or the conclusion!

Checkmate

CHESS IS ONE of the oldest games. It goes back 1,500 years to India, and from India it moved to Persia. Then the Arabs took the game and spread it all over the world.

Do you play chess? If your answer is no, then I highly encourage you to try it with a friend or family member, or you can download an app and start playing.

You set the game plan, use all your effort and all your tools, change your plan many times, and switch between the pieces. With all of that, you have one goal and a defined strategy: to win the game.

You may know the feeling when you make your last move in the game, look at the other player, and victoriously say, "Checkmate." But what is the meaning of checkmate?

Checkmate is the alteration of the Persian phrase "Shah mat," which means "The king is helpless."

Or as the Arabs translate it, "The king is dead." The word *mate* in Arabic means *died*. The word *shah* in Persian means *king*. Over time, "Shah Mat" became "checkmate."

Checkmate is not your goal in the last move of the chess game—it is your strategy from the beginning. Either you are attacking or defending. Even when you change your plan according to the dynamics of the situation, you still have one goal, and you still have one dream: that you will have the last move and will say, "Checkmate."

I don't want you to mix between your strategy and your game plan. Your game plan can change according to the situation, but it is still within the scope of your strategy. You don't change your strategy, but you change the way you apply this strategy; that is your game plan. You change your priorities according to the situation, but you always have the same strategy. It's the same as in life.

Let us see an example to simplify this concept.

Your life strategy is to be happy. As life goes on, your game plan keeps changing, but you still have the same goal, and you still follow the same strategy: is to fill your life with happiness and satisfaction. When you are young, your game plan includes going out, meeting new people, education, and so on. As you grow up, these game plans change. Your happiness will include your kids, your spouse, and even charities or civic engagements—or not!

My point is you will keep changing your game plan based on life's variables, but your strategy will still the same.

Let us talk about this life strategy. In this book, we will talk about a life strategy called the CHECKMATE strategy. In this CHECKMATE strategy, each letter represents a concept or a characteristic that you may find helpful to apply to your game of life.

Before starting, let me clarify this point again. Understanding the deep concept behind each point will help you build your life strategy, but applying the point itself is a game plan that you may or may not need to use in this phase; you may want use it later in a different phase. Think of it as a smart chess move that you know you will need to use it, but the question is when.

Before we start our journey in this book, we need to agree on few points, so let us make a deal.

1. **Don't read more than one point each day.** I am expecting you to read this book in at least nine days or more. After reading each point, take your time thinking about it from all perspectives. See how this point fits with your personality. Try to find the common ground between you and what you just read. Ask yourself, "If I was going to write about this point or explain it to someone, what would I say?" Start writing down your questions or your notes, which you will share with me after you finish the book. Even though these notes or questions might change after you finish the book, they will show you the progress you are making in understanding the theory, and they will help you develop your life game strategy.

2. **Read the stories.** In each of the nine points, you may find stories. These stories may be real or fictional. They may be from an unknown source or from a well-known source. You may already know some of these stories, it may be the first time you've heard them, or you've heard different

versions. No matter what, please read the stories, even if you know them from a different book.

Think about these stories as the ingredients you get from the market to prepare a meal. The ingredients might be the same, but the way you use them will create different meals and different flavors. You may find the same story fits in more than one point, but in each point it will have a different impact, and it will help explain different concepts. You can also think about it as watching a movie for the second time. You are not worried about the end of the movie and so can pay more attention to the small details that you didn't notice the first time.

3. **Don't jump between the points.** Okay, I know you've already browsed, or you just did so when I asked you not to do it. Let us start over. It is important to observe, digest, and analyze each point before starting the next one.

4. **If you want to change the world, start by making your bed.** The main concept of this book is that you work on yourself, not on others or on your situation. The main change starts within you. Think about this book as a guide on how to make your bed.

Now, my friend, let us start our journey.

Crying

Y ES, YOU READ it right: crying. "After a good cry, I always feel cleansed, like my heart and mind just rubbed each other backs in a warm bath." That was one of the best statements I read from "7 Good Reasons to Cry Your Eyes Out" by Therese J. Borchard.

Do you know what the safety valve is? A safety valve is a mechanism that releases excess pressure from systems when the pressure exceeds preset limits. These limits have different set values depending on the type of system. When the pressure gets too high, the safety valve will open, and all the excess pressure will be released; otherwise, this pressure will cause the system to explode!

That is with mechanical systems, but what about electric and electronic systems? In these systems, we have what is called a fuse or circuit breaker. The fuse or breaker has limits to decide the maximum current that can pass through this circuit, and if the current exceeds the limit, the fuse will break to save the rest of the circuit.

We are not that different from a mechanical or electrical system, at least from this aspect of a safety circuit. Every one of us has a different preset limit, every one of us can handle a different pressure level, and every one of us can deal with only a certain amount of current or power. That doesn't make you any better or worse than anyone else; your pressure level is not the problem. The problem is when you are not using your natural safety valve, the built-in fuse that protects you from burning. The problem is when you refuse to use the gift of crying.

This gift helps you to release all the toxic, negative feelings inside your system in the form of tears. That gift will save the system from falling down by itself!

I am not here asking you to force yourself to cry. I am asking you to stop forcing yourself to *not* cry. I am asking you to stop resisting this natural and healthy gift of releasing excess pressure and negative feelings. Release it in any form your body prefers. You can cry, scream, or do whatever your body system prefers.

Also, don't use this natural safety valve before your pressure preset limit, because you will exhaust your body without releasing the negative feelings, because the negative feelings are not there yet.

If we use the fuse example, think about yourself as an electronic circuit that can handle five amperes. The ampere is a unit to measure electric current. If you put in a fuse that can only hold three amperes, then this fuse will keep breaking all the time for no reason, whereas the system can handle more current. On the other hand, having a fuse that can handle ten amperes will not help because the whole system will break before the fuse flips! It's the same story with you: don't cry too soon, but also don't cry too late!

Don't resist releasing these toxic feelings when your body reaches the limit. Do you know why? I will let Isaac Newton answer this question. In his third law of motion, Isaac Newton stated, "For every action, there is an equal and opposite reaction." Or as I like to say it in rhyme, "Every action has a reaction, equal in magnitude and different in direction."

When I hit a wall with the ball, the wall is hitting the ball with the same force, and that is why the ball will fly back to me at almost the same speed I throw it.

Let us apply the same law on the body system. When all these negative feelings and pressures are hitting us, we need to react. If we don't react, then all these energy will stay inside the body as kinetic energy. This energy will stay inside the body until a certain moment. Then it will be released in a destructive form like anger, psychological problems, or even physiological problems like stroke, heart attack, headache, and stomachache.

Let us use Newton's laws one more time to explain this point. Remember hitting the wall with a ball? The ball will fly back to us. But if this ball is a soft rubber ball, then it will not fly back and will convert the motion energy into kinetic energy, which will transfer to heat energy. You will notice the ball starts to warm up, and with any external agent, this rubber ball can cause a fire. This rubber ball is you if you don't release the pressure.

Don't be this rubber ball—release all those negative energies!

Now is a good time to show the difference between strategy, goal, and game plan. Your strategy is to use the gift of crying to release the negative feelings and excess pressure in order to clear your mind and be able to make the right decision. That will help you to reach to the ultimate goal, which is a happy life. Your game plan is to choose when, where, and how you are going to use this tool.

When?

Use it when your body system needs it. The safety valve in any system is automatic, and so is your natural safety valve. Let it react when your body asks you to react, not after and not before. This point requires self-awareness because no one can tell you when to cry. If someone does, it's because he or she noted changes. That means you passed your limits, and your system has already started suffering from these negative energies. That will be a good guiding point for you in the future to cry earlier.

Where?

Wherever you feel it is the right place, whether in front of people, by yourself where no one can see you, or in the arms of the one you love and trust. With crying, you are releasing negative feelings, and the goal is to feel better after that. Don't release these feelings somewhere that makes you feel bad about yourself, or in front of someone who can use it against you. At the end, where are one releases feelings is different from person to another, and it's different based on the community one lives in. Even if this community believes crying is a sign of weakness. don't let that discourage you. Remember that you are doing it for yourself, not for them. You are doing it to get stronger, and you are doing it because you understand you are like any successful mechanical or electrical system, and you must have a safety valve or a fuse whose job is to save the rest of the system. Use this terminology whenever someone sees crying as a sign of weakness: simply tell this person that the system with fuses last longer because the fuses protect this system, whereas systems without safety circuits are not strong systems because once they break, they break for good!

It was one year after my graduation when I met this girl. She was everything in my life, and I was ready to give up all my dreams to be with her. Not to go through all the details, but we broke up. I didn't give myself time to heal my wounds; I didn't use my natural safety valve. For two years, I kept suffering from this relationship without moving forward. For two years, I kept telling myself that I was okay, until one day I decided to be honest with myself and be courageous enough to cry.

It takes a lot of courage to admit a failure. It takes a lot of strength to stop moving because you going nowhere. I don't remember how long I cried, but I remember how amazing I felt after that. I saw things clearly after releasing all those negative feelings. Only then did I feel honest with myself when I said, "I am okay." With this clear mind and clear heart, I met my real soul mate, my wife.

It took me two years to recover and to use my natural safety circuit, crying, because I'd grown up in a community that saw crying as a sign of weakness. I don't want you to suffer the same fate and waste time and energy. People are a mix of logic and feelings, and if your feelings are not clear, your thoughts will not be clear either. Your tears are there for a reason. Don't ignore them!

How?

Cry, scream, jump, breathe. Every system has its own safety valve, and every person has a way to release these negative feelings. Find yours and use it!

Healthy

To be healthy doesn't only mean being in a good shape, working out every day, or following nutrition guides. By doing all of that, you will have a healthy body. And yes, the healthy body will help your brain to function more effectively and will save you from falling into the vicious circle of depression. However, the concept of being healthy doesn't start and end with your metabolism and how to burn fats and control calories. Let us find out more about this concept.

One of the healthy living style tips is to avoid junk food as much as you can, but what about junk thoughts and junk feelings? What about avoiding useless conversations and stressful situations? What about avoiding relationships with people who are causing you stress and pain more than love and happiness?

Sometimes it is hard to break these relationships with some people who may be close relatives, friends, or even a long-term workmate, so in a case like this, what can one do?

Think of this situation. You stop eating your favorite type of food because it is not healthy, but you still can watch this food. I can look at a slice of pizza for hours, but I am not going to take a single bite of it; it is not going to end up inside my body. Now apply the same concept in your relationships with people who have a negative impact on you. You still can see them, talk with them, and listen to them, but their thoughts, feelings, and negative impact will not end up into your mind and will not affect your mood. How?

Let us use the same example of the pizza slice. If you leave yourself starving, then this pizza slice will definitely end up inside your body. If you eat a healthy meal, then you can keep looking at the pizza slice without eating it; you are not hungry, and there is no space inside you for this slice.

The same concept applies when dealing with these negative people. Fill your mind and your heart with positive thoughts and feelings, and then there is no space for their negative thoughts! Do this by watching a movie, reading a book, or listening to your favorite music. You can meditate, pray, close your eyes, and go to your happy place. Choose whatever makes you feel positive energy, and then there will be no room for others' negative energy.

"But what if those people surprised me before getting ready for them, and out of nowhere they get into my mind with their negative energy?" you ask.

So you are saying, "What if I have to eat the pizza slice?"

The answer is simple: work out. As you know, working out helps your body to burn excess calories and increase your metabolism so your body will get rid of excess fats and toxins. Working out will also help your body to get rid of all negative feelings and thoughts. Go for a run, or practice your hobby (whether it is a physical hobby like basketball or a mental hobby like chess). Any of these activities will burn the negative energies and get you back in shape.

Do not meet a good friend and talk with her about these negative feelings. You have to try your best to release the negative energy by yourself.

Why?

Let us use the same concept about eating healthy. Eating a healthy meal after eating junk food will not help you to lose weight. It's the same thing about having a conversation with a good friend after you get stuffed with all those negative energies, The last thing you want is to be a negative person by exposing those negative thoughts to your friends.

Think of these negative feelings as a bad meal that your body needs to get rid of it. Can you do that in front of a friend? Would you like to talk with your friends about your visits to the bathroom?

Even if you talk with a good friend about these negative feelings, don't do that while you still have these feelings. First get rid of them, and then you can talk with your friend about these feelings as a learning experience. Always shine, and always be the one who speaks positively.

One of the recommendations to have healthy lifestyle is to practice yoga. What is your first thought when you hear the term? Flexibility. Your body needs to be flexible in order to have a healthy lifestyle. It's the same as your thoughts: your ideas and your feelings need to be flexible to have a healthy lifestyle.

Your body's flexibility goes on different levels depending on how long you practice yoga. These flexibility levels are different from one person to the next depending on the nature of the body. It's the same as your thoughts, feelings, and ideas. Flexibility will be different between people, and it is your responsibility to find your point of flexibility. which works with your nature. You should not be too hard on yourself so that life breaks you, but you also should not be too flexible so that life squeezes you. You need to find your equilibrium point where you can keep your ideas and morals under control.

Do not get confused and mix your ideas and habits with your morals. Your ideas, your thoughts, and your habits need to be flexible. We are living in a dynamic world, and we have to adapt to survive, but your morals need to stay rigid in order to keep your identity.

To make this concept clear, think of yourself as a tree. Your ideas, thoughts, and habits are the tree's branches and leaves, and your morals are the roots.

Let us use yoga terms. Your muscles and ligaments need to be flexible, but your bones need to be strong and rigid to keep your body in shape.

Let me give you an example. I was born and raised in Egypt and then moved to the United States. Living in the United States exposed me to the real meaning of diversity, feeling the other side, and seeing situations from different perspectives before taking any action. I had to change some of my thoughts and habits, but at the same time I kept my morals because without my morals, I was not the same person.

For example, In Egypt when a man and woman meet each other, they shake hands, and in conservative places they may salute without a handshake. When two men meet each other, they hug and kiss on the cheek. I had to change this habit when I moved to the United States; when I meet a friend, whether male or female, I hug this friend if the person is okay with that. Does that mean I lost my identity and my morals? No. It means I am adapting a new habit using my flexibility, but my morals are still the same, and that is expressing my feelings to my friend, respecting my friend, and being loyal to my friend.

I use the same flexibility when I go back to Egypt, and I salute females or shake hands. But I am still keeping the same morals!

Confused? You may say, "But to keep changing like that would make me a hypocrite, and I'd lose my identity!"

Remember, your identity is your morals and beliefs, not your habits. Changing your habits based on the people and the location will not make you a hypocrite but will make you flexible and tactful.

One of the common mistakes people fall into when they move from their home country to a different place is they mix between their morals and their habits. They lose their morals, thinking they are adapting, and that makes them exceed their point of flexibility and lose their identity; they end up squeezed. Or they keep their habits, thinking they are protecting their morals, and that makes them very stiff; they end up living in a bubble. You need to avoid these two extremes, and you can do so by defining what are your habits and what are your morals. Let your thoughts, ideas, and habits be as flexible as they need to be based on where you live, but keep your morals rigid and strong because your identity is defined by your morals, not by your habits.

People don't feel you are a stranger and don't belong to them because of your morals, but because of your habits.

"But my habits represents my cultures and morals!" you say.

Here is the silver lining, the questions that you need to think about it. You are the only one who can answer them. Is this habit based on beliefs and morals, or it is simply something you grew up doing? Will Is letting go of this habit impact your identity, or will help you to represent it and enjoy it in a different way?

Keep practicing, keep reading, keep listening, and keep observing—then the decision is yours!

Let me tell you a story about these young couples who just got married. One day they were in the kitchen, frying fish for lunch, when the wife held the fish and cut off the tail and the head before putting the fish in the frying pan. Then she fried the head and the tail!

The husband looked to her, surprised, and asked, "Why did you cut off the tail and the head?"

She looked at him astonished and said, "What kind of question is that? You can't fry the fish with the head and the tail. That would poison the fish!"

The husband said, "But you're still frying the head and the tail!"

The wife replied, "If I didn't cut the head and the tail, the whole fish will be poisoned. It's not the same case when I fry them alone."

The husband found his wife very stubborn, but she would not let go the idea of cutting off the fish head and tail, so he let it go. Then one day, they were visiting his mother-in-law, and he asked her, "What is the story about cutting off the fish head and tail before frying it?"

The mother-in-law answered with a smile, "Oh, dear, we grew up poor and had only one small frying pan. A fish will not fit in the pan, so I used to cut off the head and the tail. I didn't want my kids to feel bad, so I told them if we didn't cut off the head and the tail, the fish would be poisoned!"

How many beliefs could turn into habits due to the way we grow up, and how many are real beliefs? You are the one who can answer that. It is up to you to question every habit and belief and decide where you need to be fixable and where you need to be rigid.

The core of all cultures is the same; the core of all morals is the same. The way we represent them will have differences based on where and how we grew up!

For example, stealing is wrong in all cultures, but the retribution is different based on where you live. Respecting seniors is a fact in all cultures, but sitting cross-legged in the presence of a senior is a habit that may offended her in some cultures! Act your morals and your culture, but if you find a way to practice these beliefs in a way that matches your new community, you will enjoy it much more than getting stuck with the same habits you grew up with!

Think of morals as what you want to say, and the habit is the language you are using. You can say what you believe, but with different languages rather than the language you grow up speaking. You will still be able to deliver the same meaning to your audience, but only if you speak a language that your audience can understand!

Another valuable tip to having a healthy lifestyle is to get a regular checkup and blood work so you know all your body organs are in good shape. Even if they seem to be working good, it's the same concept as when you take your car for preventive maintenance. We need to apply the same concept to our thoughts, feelings, ideas, principles, habits, and even beliefs. They may seem to be working well, but you will never be sure until you check them.

Once in a while, go for a conversation you always try to avoid because you don't have a good argument. See how you progress. Maybe you will change some of your thoughts, or maybe you will be surer about your beliefs!

Read a book about something you disagree with it. For example, if you believe in Creation, then you need to read a book about evolution and see how strong your beliefs are. Maybe you will change your mind, or maybe you will keep the same beliefs. Perhaps you will come up with some theory that links both beliefs!

Have a conversation with yourself and then with your friends. Don't be scared by the truth if it is different than what you thought. Read, talk, listen, and discuss. There are no taboos; respect all points of view because every right has something wrong, and every wrong has something right. Be the filter that passes the right from everything to your soul and drops the wrong. Be a fruit salad rather than just one kind of fruit.

Don't mix this point with the point about avoiding negative conversations or people. There are differences between different points of view and negative points of view, between argument and fighting, between thinking negatively and showing the negative side of a situation.

Remember that when you get a checkup, you should choose a good doctor. When you take your car for maintenance, you choose a good mechanic, and the same principle applies when you have a conversation or read a book to check your thoughts and beliefs.

Live healthy in all aspects—body, mind, heart, ideas, habits, and feelings!

Education

"Do not give me a fish; instead, teach me how to fish." You will find this aphorism all over the world. No matter the language or the culture, no matter the differences between countries, you will find the same quote because they all agree on the value of education.

We all understand the importance of education, whether academic, self-taught, or whatever way you decided to educate yourself.

My first year at Cairo University, Egypt, was 1992, and I studied systems and biomedical engineering. I still remember my math professor at our first lecture. He talked with us about everything—except math. It's a lecture that I will never forget because it changed my life perspective! I still remembering him saying, "A successful person is the one who knows everything about one thing, and knows one thing about everything."

You need to be the expert on one thing. No matter what it is, no matter how small or big this thing, no matter how simple or complicated, you need to be the specialist, the expert. Whenever we mention this thing, your name will jump on the table. Whenever we mention your name, this thing will jump on the table. To that degree, you need to be an expert on that thing. Again, it doesn't matter how big or small this thing is.

For example, if I said, "Martial arts," you will find yourself thinking about Bruce Lee. If I said, "Bruce Lee," you will start thinking about martial arts. But how many of us will think about Bruce Lee if we are talking about acting, even though we all know him from movies? To that degree, you need to master one thing, as Bruce Lee mastered martial arts, as Albert Eisenstein mastered physics, or as McDonald's mastered the cheeseburger.

At the same time, without losing your knowledge and your reputation regarding the one thing you mastered, you will need to learn one thing about everything. When I say one thing, I don't literally mean only one thing, but you don't need to master your education about everything. Actually, you can't do that, but you can have some knowledge about everything, and you can have an idea about everything. When I say *everything*, I mean as much as you can. There will be always something you don't know about it, and this will be a new learning opportunity.

Let me explain this idea in a different way. How do you like an amazing masterpiece tableau with a cheap frame or without any frame? You still like it and could pay a lot of money to get it, but you still need a good frame to represent it! This is the same about an expert on one thing without any knowledge about anything else, or minor knowledge about different things.

How do you like a cheap tableau in a very expensive frame? Probably you will not bother buying it! This is the similar someone who is intellectual in different fields but without a field of experience.

The masterpiece tableau needs a piece of art and a frame; only then will it attract everyone to see how amazing it is. As I said before, the piece of art has its value no matter the frame, but what we are talking about now is how we are representing this piece of art (how you represent yourself as an expert in a field surrounded by knowledge in different fields).

Let us play a game to make this concept clear. You can play this game with family members, friends, or workmates. Let everyone have a pen and paper. Randomly mention one of the player's names, and let the others write the first impression that pops into their minds when they hear the name. Collect the anonymous papers and analyze the data. See how many of them mentioned the person's field of experience, and see what else they mentioned. Play the game with different groups and at different times, and you can see how you progress and how different people are seeing you. That will help you to identify the value of the tableau (your field of experience) and the value of the frame (your general knowledge).

I give credit for this game idea to a workmate and a friend, Nader Abbas, may he rest in peace. He once told me, "You are a good engineer, but when we mention your name in any meeting, we talk about how funny you are, or your stories about dating girls—not how good you are as engineer." That was one of the best constructive criticisms I ever received, and it was a shocking moment!

I was shocked because even when I knew the quote from my math professor many years ago I needed to know everything about one thing and one thing about everything, I didn't apply it on myself. I didn't live the quote and turn it into a part of my character, a part of my lifestyle. After Nader said this, I paused to reevaluate myself and learn what was missing. That was when I came up with this game as a source of feedback to measure my progress regarding how I represent myself to the world.

Two years later, my field of experience became my last name. Whenever they mentioned my name, they mentioned my work skills. Then they talked about my different skills, and because of that, I had the opportunity to move from Egypt to the United States. Because of that, I am writing this book that you are reading now!

What really amazed me during these two years between changing my strategy and moving to the United States was that I didn't do anything extra. I was working and studying the same number of hours, and I was still hanging out with friends. I simply redefined my priorities, I redefined my goals and the focus on my conversations, which in turn changed the way I presented myself. That opened the door to a lifetime opportunity!

I would have never moved to the United States and had my life changed without that conversation with my friend Nader. I would never have had the chance to write this book you are reading now if he hadn't cared to give me this constructive criticism. Thanks, Nader Abbas. May you rest in peace and be rewarded for all your good manners and principles.

Now, let us move to another point, which is being intellectual and having good knowledge about everything. We have been using the example of the tableau, so let us now talk about the frame.

First, let us define the differences between having general knowledge and being intellectual. Everyone has general knowledge not to be successful but to survive. These days, with all the informative media surrounding us, general knowledge is not a privilege—it is a must.

But only distinguished people upgrade themselves from the general knowledge phase to the intellectual phase. How? It's simple: they read. Invest your time and get information by reading from different sources, not just by watching or reading from one source!

When you watch informative media like TV, or when you're browsing the internet, you are only seeing the tip of the iceberg, which is less than 5 percent. You are getting the information the way the media sees it, not the way your mind and your heart see it. You are getting the information coated with their flavor. It is like buying a fast food meal: all you can do is to eat it.

When you invest your time in reading the information from different sources, you are cooking your own meal. You are searching for the ingredient and cooking it the way you like it, the way you feel it and understand it. Savor the information and add the flavors of your feelings, your thoughts, and your ideas. At the end, you will not be a parrot repeating what you hear. You will be a human with an opinion.

People may have the same information, but they will have different points of view based on the way they digest these information, and that will create a healthy environment of constructive discussion and brainstorming rather than group thinking. That will make each one of us unique. If life is a chessboard, we will not be the pawns. Instead, we will be pawns, rooks, bishops, knights, queens, and kings. We will create diversity, with diverse points of views!

Don't fall into the trap of "I am intellectual and you are not." The moment you think you're better than someone because you are intellectual is the moment you should realize that you are not as intellectual as you thought. This has nothing to do with humbleness, Although there is a proportional relationship between your level of education and your humility, the reason for avoiding this trap is that when you think you are more intellectual than others, that is when you stop listening, stop reading, and (without noticing it) downgrade yourself from the intellectual phase to the general knowledge phase.

Don't mix between humility and putting yourself down. Be proud that you have your own thoughts and ideas. Be proud that you search for information from different sources but at the same time respect all points of view, as long as it is within a constructive discussion.

We talked about the tableau and the frame, and now we need to cover one more point before we wrap up this section of our CHECKMATE strategy theory. We need to talk about experience. How will you gain experience to master your field of specialty?

One of the approaches is to read about former colleagues' experiences in your field of interest. Another approach is to practice the situation by yourself and gain hands-on experience. If you are fostering this approach, note that experience doesn't come as a grant from situations. You need to observe, evaluate the whole situation, and take notes.

After every task or situation, you need to stop and ask yourself the STAR questions.

What was the **S**ituation?

What was your **T**ask?

What was the **A**ction you took?

What was the **R**esult?

Based on the answers, you will decide to act the same way you did when you face this situation again, or you will follow a different approach and take a different action, You will decide whether the results were satisfactory or whether you need to reach out for more tools, resources, thoughts, and ideas to get better results.

Most job interviews use the behavior interview, which is based on the STAR technique. It is useful to write notes to yourself whenever you face a situation at work or in life. Ask yourself the four STAR questions. Spending some time with observation will save you more time when you face a similar situation in the future.

This practice will help you on any job interview, because you will have many stories to tell and many areas of the interview to cover—not just with thoughts and ideas but with personal stories that will make a great impact on your future employer!

Now let us sum up this point in few simple equations

Information + Informative Media = General Knowledge

General Knowledge + Reading and Browsing Different Resources = Intellectual

Continuance Research + Self-learning and Academic Education = Field of Specialty

Field of Specialty + Experience = Distinguished in the Field

Intellectual + Distinguished in the Field = Success

Communication

THE MYTH SAYS, "The number thirteen is a sign of bad luck." I believe this myth is true only because *communication* is thirteen letters, and if you miss these thirteen letters, your life will be a vicious circle of bad luck situations.

We all know the importance of communication. We value the importance of delivering our ideas and feelings in proper and clear ways using different techniques, which we call the art of communication. On a daily basis, you will meet people with different communication skills. Some of them are beginners, and some of them are professionals, but I assure you that only successful people you met or read about are good communicators.

Let us try to understand the meaning of communication. When we talk about communication, we are talking about verbal communication because you are using your vocabulary to transfer your ideas. You can also have nonverbal communication because you are using your gestures, your tone, your facial expressions, and even your silence to deliver a message.

Communication is like a coin because it has two sides: talking and listening, writing and reading.

The art of communication is not just how to deliver your ideas. It's also how to receive others' ideas. To master the art of communication, you need to move from the hearing phase to the listening phase. You have two ears and one mouth, so if you are talking more than listening, then you are against the nature of communication.

Let me tell you a story. In 2013 I joined a toastmaster club, which is a nonprofit educational organization that teaches public speaking and leadership skills. I was honored to listen to one of the greatest speakers, Robert Mackenzie, who passed away on September 27, 2014, may he rest in peace.

Robert was giving an impromptu speech: "What if there is no heaven?" He was talking about hope and belief, and he wrapped up his speech by saying, "If there is no heaven, then …" He fell down on the floor.

For ten seconds, no one moved. Then one of the club members broke the silence and stood up to check him. Robert had lost his conscious, and his head had knocked the corner of the wall and started bleeding. He had a heart pacemaker, and it stopped and restarted again, causing a disturbance in his heart, which made him lose consciousness.

This situation shocked me, and I kept blaming myself that I was not listing to his speech. I thought I was listening to him, but in reality I was not.

If I was really listening to him, I would have noticed the changes in his facial expressions. I would have noticed his legs were stumbling. I would have known that the falling down was not a part of his speech. I actually loved his speech to the degree I'd started to digest it before it ended. I started to have conclusions in my mind, and my mind told me that the falling down would be the perfect end of this speech, which meant I was listening to my mind and not to his speech. I was interrupting him not by talking but by building conclusions before he'd finished.

Since this accident, I have trained myself to deeply listen to the conversations, and I forced my mind to stop building conclusions, feelings, and thoughts until the end of the conversation. This is not easy and requires practice and observation, but the results will be outstanding. The results will make you on the top of any situation, enhancing your reactions and awareness.

When someone is speaking, he uses verbal and nonverbal communication skills to deliver his feelings, ideas, and information. The goal is to deliver this information to your mind and to your heart. That is why keeping your mind busy with anything, even with building a conclusion to the conversation, is actually a kind of interruption.

Now, don't mix up keeping your mind busy analyzing and understanding the received information, which is active listening, and keeping your mind busy with building conclusions, which is passive listening. Always watch yourself to know whether you are really listening to the speaker or are listening to your mind giving the same speech. Are you noticing the speaker movements, and do these movements and gestures match his speech? Say to yourself, "If I was evaluating this speech, what would I say to him?" Write down notes of the speech. These are some techniques I use to keep myself as an active listener.

You may ask, "What if I am listening to a bad presentation, and the speaker can't deliver his message? How can I stay an active listener?" You can use any poor presentation as a learning opportunity. Get a pen and paper and write down the pros and cons of this presentation. What do you need to avoid if you are giving the same presentation? Then write down this golden rule: "There is no absolute bad." There must be something good in this presentation, some new information, new technique, or new idea. Find this thing. If speakers or writers didn't deliver the information as they should, don't do like them. Do your job as an active listener or active reader. If they didn't communicate as they should, you will communicate in a proper way, and you will learn from their mistakes.

Don't let a bad speech turn you into a bad listener. Don't let a bad book turn you into bad reader. If you don't like what you are reading so far, hang on and keep reading.

So far, we've talked about communication with others as verbal and nonverbal. We also talked about the importance of listening and how to be an active listener. Now we will talk about the core of communication: communication with yourself.

The key to mastering the art of communication with others is to communicate with yourself. It all starts within you. The art of communication starts when you start looking at yourself not as one person but as an organization. The board members of this organization are your heart, your brain, your mind, and your soul.

As the owner of this organization, you are deciding which one of these board members will be the CEO—who will represent this organization and shape the organization personality. Different members in this organization are your eyes, your legs, your hands, your lungs, et cetera.

Now that you are about to look at yourself from a different perspective, look at yourself as *we*, not as *I*.

Why?

First, you will never feel alone because you are not one anymore—you are a whole organization. Fostering this concept will save you from falling into depression or feeling lonely. Second, you will feel more powerful and more organized. Third, you will have better understanding and a variety of solutions to the problems you are facing. Because you can easily identify the source of this problem within the organization, you will be able to define whether your heart, your mind, your soul, or your brain is the source of the problem, or whether any other members in the organization (your body, for example) is not listening to your brain and not responding to a workout. Maybe there is a conflict between the brain's orders and the heart's feelings; then you will start to think outside the box. Maybe your problem is because your heart is the CEO, and you need your brain to lead. That will help you to simulate the situation from a different perspective, and it will make you think and act in a different way.

As you set the concept of looking to yourself as an organization, let me ask you a question. What is the key factor of success in any organization? It's communication.

Increasing the level of transparency and reducing rumors will help any organization avoid chaotic situations, and that will help this organization to communicate more effectively.

The key factor to communicating effectively with the world is to communicate with yourself. How can you communicate with yourself? By using the concept of the four Cs: conversation, control, calm, and constructive criticism.

Before we start talking about the four Cs, I need you to close your eyes and see yourself from the organization's perspective. Answer this question: Who is the CEO? Is it your heart, your mind, your soul, your brain, or more than one?

Now, let us start talking about the four Cs.

Conversation

In any successful organization, there are periodical meetings between board members, and with the concept of an organization you need to have these kind of meetings and start the conversation with your board members: your heart, your mind, your brain, and your soul.

Give yourself fifteen minutes every night to let every member talk about its day.

Ask your heart about all the feelings you felt today, whether love, hate, peace, or anger. Ask your heart what you need to improve on, what feelings you need to reduce, and how that affects you.

Ask your brain about all the ideas and information you had today, and how they will help your organization. Remember that you are the organization.

Let your soul speak and give a feedback about all you have been through during the day.

Check with your mind about how it was affected by all the events during the day, and how it is accepting all the new ideas and concepts.

Having this conversation on a daily basis will help you identify small problems before they get big, and it will also help you isolate the source of the problem, define the reasons for the problem, and set the proper game plan to solve the problem.

Remember when I asked you to close your eyes and figure out who is the CEO of your organization? This CEO is defining your personality. Either you are a person who uses your feelings as a primary indicator, or you use your ideas and thoughts, or you use your beliefs, or you use your intuition. Based on that, you will see your daily events in this daily meeting from one of these perspectives.

Now, let us play a game. Change the CEO. If you are a person who uses your heart to judge situations, you will find your heart leading you while your feelings are controlling the conversation, and that flavors your ideas and thoughts, which will make you always see situations from one side. Start to use your brain as the CEO, perform your daily activities, and check whether you see things differently. Then try your soul, then your mind. This will help you to see the same situations from different views, and it may also show you problems you will never see if the leader of your organization is your heart all the time!

Switching the CEO means switching the prescribed glasses that you use to see your day. It means switching the way you think about things, the way you judge situations and create solutions.

You probably do this without noticing—something you may call "thinking outside the box" or looking for alternatives solutions. Doing the same thing under the new concept that you are a whole organization and not just one person will make things taste and look different, and you will enjoy doing it on a daily basis!

Following these fifteen-minute daily meetings, you will need to set a longer meeting once every week or every month, depending on your schedule and your day-to-day activities. It is important to set a time for this one-hour meeting on a weekly or monthly basis so you can ask the board members a very important question: "How far are we from our goal?"

I am assuming that you have a goal to achieve. Everyone has a goal in life—actually, everyone has many goals in life. Sometimes these goals are so clear and obvious to the degree that you forget about them, and you can easily get distracted.

For example, when you enrolled in some training courses, your goal was not to finish these courses; your goal was to learn these courses so you could use them in your work, and that would help you get a better position to enhance your financial situation so you could buy a house.

Your goal was to buy a house, your action plan was to increase your income from your work, and your tools were to get extra training courses. If you didn't keep reminding yourself about your goal, you would get distracted and get things mixed up between your goal, your action plan, and your tools. These tools were simply subgoals and were not the main goal.

You need to keep this image clear all the time. You need all your board members up to date, and they must agree and understand the goal. Discuss any changes in your ideas, feelings, or thoughts that may distract you from achieving your goal. That is why you need to have this monthly or weekly meeting. You need to make sure that every board member is using its tools and skills to steer the organization in the right direction to reach your goal.

At these meetings, after you make sure that you are still focusing on your goal and still feel the same way about your goal, you need to measure your progress from the last meeting. Are you moving forward or backward? Are you focusing on achieving your subgoals, or did you get distracted and bored? Let us use the training courses example. Your subgoal is to understand these courses, not just finish them, because your next step is to implement these courses in your business. You need to ask yourself these questions at your monthly meetings.

- Am I really getting the maximum information from these courses?
- Do I feel bored, or am I enjoying them?
- Am I on track timewise, do I need to work faster, or do I need to slow down?
- Am I distracted and rushing, or am I focusing on my subgoals and seeing them as a step in my action plan to achieve my goal of buying a house?
- Are there any changes in the circumstances that require I change the subgoals or the action plan to achieve my goal?

This is a very important point. Let us use the same example and assume you changed your position or your career. Now you don't need these training courses to enhance your financial situation. If you are focusing on your goal, then you will drop these courses and start doing something else to achieve your goal. But if you get distracted and confused between the goal and the subgoals, then you will keep working on these courses, which are now consuming your money and your time and are not helping you to achieve your goal.

- Do I still feel the same about the main goal?

This point is also very important. What drive you to achieve your goal are your feelings, not your ideas and thoughts. That is why it is very important to have all of them walking in the same direction. Don't ignore any small changes in your feelings—work on them right away. Don't force your feelings to stay in the same direction;

Wessam Eldein

first understand them, and then ask yourself why you are not seeing your goal the same way you used to see it. Why are you not excited about your goal in the same way you used to be? Is that because of solid data indicating that your goal is not achievable in the preset time frame? Or is it because you are not excited about this goal any longer, or you had changes in your life and now are pursuing another goal?

It is very important that no matter the decision you take after this meeting, your feelings, your thoughts, your ideas, and your background are all moving in the same direction toward your goal or to a new goal.

If you decide to drop a main goal for another goal, know the real reasons behind that. Have all the board members agree on this decision and then get to work on a new game plan and subgoals. Always make sure that all the board members are working in harmony to avoid any confusion, which can cause depression.

These periodic conversations will define any problem or conflict of interest in the early stages, saving you from wasting time and effort.

Let us use another example to wrap up this point. Your goal is to get a job in an international company in France. Your action plan is to learn French, to get certified in some IT courses, and to save some money for flight expenses.

Your subgoals are as follows.

- Apply to a community college to get the courses.
- Pass the language courses.

- Work on different jobs for a few months to save money.

While you are working on this action plan, you meet this girl and fall in love with her. She doesn't want you to move to Europe. Now it is a time for a board meeting to discuss the new changes.

Ask yourself if you still feel the same about your goal. Ask your mind and your soul how they feel about this conflict. Ask your heart and your brain about their feelings and impressions. Work together on an action plan to convince your girlfriend about your goal, if you still feel the same about your goal. Be honest with yourself. At the end, if you can't reach a decision, then you may need to vote and see what your mind, brain, soul, and heart say. Listen to the majority.

Then change the CEO, think again, and vote again. That way you are seeing the problem from all sides. Compare all sides, and you will come with a decision, or a new action plan, or a new goal. No matter the end result, your heart, your mind, your brain, and your soul will walk in the same direction in harmony, based on democracy. You as the organization's official speaker will not speak or take any action without the approval of all board members. Write down your decision and mark it with the date so that in the future, if you feel confused, you can remind yourself about this board meeting and why you took this decision.

Remember that the conversation starts within yourself.

Control

"Everything is under control." How does that sound? Sounds great, right?

Let me start with the bad news: that sentence is completely wrong because there is no way to have everything under control.

For example, if you are driving your car and your friend in the passenger seat asks you to slow down, you will say, "Don't worry; everything is under control." You are exaggerating because you are controlling the car, but you are not controlling other drivers, and you are not controlling their actions and reactions.

If you are playing a video game, then you are controlling the character you are playing. You are controlling your reactions, but you are not controlling the electricity and the chance of a power failure. You are not controlling a sudden glitch in your video game or the console.

You will never control everything, but you can control what you are communicating. You need to set up a communication level with things or people. Then through this communication, you can start the control phase.

If we go back to the car example, you are controlling the car because you are communicating with the car. You are listening to the engine, you checked the tires, and you are watching the speedometer to monitor your speed. You checked the oil, and you feel the steering wheel. You are communicating with the car, and that is why you are controlling the car.

To create a level of communication with other drivers, all cars have rearview and side mirrors. Lights and honking can also communicate your actions to other drivers, and that will create a level of control. Some cars will have sensors to stop the car if the distance to other cars or obstacles is too close, and that is another kind of communication to increase the level of control. It's the same with playing a video game. You are communicating with the game, you know the moves, and you know all the key functions. You are controlling the game because you are communicating with it. You've practiced, practicing leads to progress, progress leads to perfection, and perfection will guarantee you control—but only what you can communicate!

Based on this analysis, control is about communication, and the moment you lose communication, you will lose control. But how and where does the controlling process start? In other words, if we go back to the car example, what comes before controlling the steering wheel, the brakes, and the RPM?

Before all of that, you must control yourself—your rhythm and your reactions. Without that emotional stability, you cannot accomplish your control over anything. This is the good news and is our golden rule: "To control anything and to have the upper hand in any situation, you first need to control yourself. The control process starts with communication, so controlling yourself will start by communicating with yourself."

Let us talk about communicating with yourself from the perspective of control. In the beginning, we talked about listening as a major section in the communication process. Do you listen to yourself? Do you listen to your heartbeat when you get worried and confused, or you ignore these feelings? Do you try to calm yourself and give yourself some time to express your feelings, or do you give yourself reasons and data and facts to convince yourself about your next action?

Let me ask you another question. Did you find out who is your CEO? Is it your heart, your brain, your mind, or your soul?

Why am I asking this question again? Because if you didn't find your CEO, then you are not listening to yourself, and therefore you are not communicating with yourself. That means you are not controlling yourself, which makes you lose control in any situation.

Your CEO will define your personality, which will lead you to the right language when you are communicating with yourself.

Yes, many people lose their self-control and live with panic and tension because they didn't pause for five minutes and weren't sincere with themselves to answer the question, "Who is my CEO?" Note that it's not "Who would I like to be my CEO?" You don't want to cheat yourself, and you don't want to be in continuous conflict between who you are and who you think you should be. These people will communicate with themselves in a wrong language, and the result is no communication.

Let us assume that your CEO is your heart, which means you are a person about feelings, emotions, and people more than thoughts, ideas, facts, beliefs, and morals. You think you should be more about morals and beliefs to make it rigid because they represent your identity, and for that you think the CEO should be your soul.

What you need to do in this situation is to give yourself sometime, calm down, and let your heart express all these emotions. Ignoring these feelings and focusing only on beliefs will cause miscommunication and as a result losing control.

What if the CEO is your brain, and you feel panic?

Here, the situation is different. Your heart is panicking as a reaction of your brain seeing something wrong. Then you need to talk to your brain with the language your brain can understand, which is data, facts, and reasons.

The moment your brain is convinced, your heart will calm down.

Choose the language based on your CEO.

That is why I will keep saying you should find out who your CEO is and then use its language. If your heart is the CEO, then use feelings and emotions. If your soul is the CEO, then use beliefs. If your mind is the CEO, then use your thoughts and ideas. If your brain is the CEO, then use facts and data. It is not wrong to have any of these as the CEO, because there is nothing wrong with being yourself. What is wrong is talking to yourself as someone else, communicating with yourself in a language you don't understand, and knowing all the people around you but not stopping for five minutes to know yourself.

After you use the right language and communicate with yourself, you are controlling yourself, and you've successfully accomplished the first phase in controlling situations around you. But what about the things you can't control? Simply don't worry about them. Because we can't control these things, we use the term "risk factor."

Let us first explain why there are things out of control. You don't have a level of communication with these things. Let us go back to the car example. When you are driving your car, you can't control other drivers' actions and reactions because you have a very limited communication level with them, like the turn signals or honking. That is why you need to have a risk factor when you are making any decision that includes out-of-control elements. For example, you can't suddenly turn left or right without calculating your risk factors to see the chance that you may hit any of the cars around you—or that any of these cars may hit each other based on your sudden movement.

Also, if you know that you and your car can control the situation when driving ninety miles per hour, you still need to drive seventy miles per hour because you can't control other drivers or the road itself!

But if you are on a racetrack, where you know the road and are communicating in a better way with other drivers, then you can increase your speed to the max limits to win the race. The same driver with the same car can't drive with the same speed on a different road and with other drivers because he doesn't have the same level of communication with all factors.

Let us wrap up this point by emphasizing that communicating with yourself is the key to controlling yourself, and controlling yourself is the first step to controlling everything—but only the everything with which you can communicate.

Therefore it is not "Everything is under control." It is "Everything I communicate with is under control."

Calm

In this section, I want you to see the strong relationship between communication and calm, as well as how they lead to each other in a way that you can't tell which one comes first. That leads us to the question, "Does successful communication lead to calmness, or does calmness lead to successful communication?"

What we can confirm is that you can't have one without the other. You can't communicate if you are not calm, and you will not be calm unless you are communicating and controlling the situation—starting with yourself!

Communication and calmness exchange the roles; they both are the reason and the result.

Your level of calmness is always being tested, and you need to keep an eye on it and work on enhancing this level. That will not happen by being optimistic, and it definitely will not happen by being pessimistic. It will happen by being realistic. Be honest with yourself, and face what you can achieve and what you can't, what you can control and what you can't. Then find your inner peace by following these three rules.

Rule 1: "You are better than anyone on Earth in something—and anyone walking on Earth is better than you in something."

Let us play this game. Think of anyone whom you see as a role model, or as a very successful person. You will find you're better than this person in something. You may be more knowledgeable or much stronger, or you can play a certain game better than him. You may sing better than him, or you are a better actor. In the end, you definitely have something this person doesn't have.

Now, think about anyone you feel that you are better than, and you will find this person is better than you in something. Again, this person may be faster than you. She may know more about fashion than you, or she is calmer in stressed situations.

How do you feel now? You feel more balanced and calmer. You feel humble, and at the same time you have more self-confidence.

The secret of calmness is to find this balance between self-confidence and humility. The secret of calmness is to believe that you are better than anyone, and anyone is better than you.

Rule 2: "You can lose your temper only when you have nothing to lose."

This is the rule you need to remember in any argument, situation, or discussion. The last thing you need to lose is your temper. You can show your feelings, you can show your anger, and you can shout and scream if the situation requires these techniques. But deep inside yourself, you are calm, you know how to control yourself, and you are communicating with yourself. You have this game plan that may include showing your anger to win a point or to defend your position, but because you are deeply calm, you know when to switch off this anger.

For example, when one of my kids does something wrong and the situation requires an assertive action, I may look upset and give my kid a hard tone, but deep inside I am very calm. This is my first check before I start a behavior discussion with the kid: "Am I calm?" If the answer is yes, then I start to work on the game plan, which may include some tone and anger act. If I have a doubt about my calmness, I don't get involved with the kids or with any other activities.

Calmness is your first check before any daily activities. Use the anger as a technique—don't let the anger use you. If you let anger use you, it will turn to rage, and rage is something no one can control.

Rule 3: "Don't let your mood control your attitude."

Let me tell you a story. You may know it, but a reminder will not hurt. Once upon a time, a father noticed his son was angry all the time. The kid lost his temper for any reason, and then he felt sorry and apologized. The father talked to his son many times about how important it was to keep under control, but the kid never got the idea.

His father decided to teach his son a lesson in a different way. He gave his son a pile of nails and said, "Son, I want you to take one of these nails and hammer it into this concrete wall every time you act angry. Let me know when you finish all the nails."

In the first day, the son hammered twenty nails, but it was a very hard job to hammer all these nails into a concrete wall. On the next day, to save some of his energy, the son tried to control his temper as much as he could. Day after day, the son became calmer and more in control.

The son went back to his father and said, "Father, I still have nails with me, but it has been days, and I haven't needed to hammer nails into the wall."

The father said, "Now I want you to take out one nail every day you feel calm and in control of your mood."

Day after day and week after week, the son took out a nail every day he felt calm and controlled his temper. Finally the son took out all the nails and proudly went back to his father.

"Father, I took out all the nails."

The father said, "Great. Let us check the wall. Look, my son. You took out all the nails from the wall, but look to all these holes in the concrete wall. This wall will never be the same before you hammered these nails. Likewise, people will never be the same after you hammer them with the nails of hard words and rage, even after you take out these nails by apologizing."

Don't let your mood control your attitude. Don't make your words like sharp nails.

As Ambrose Bierce, the American writer, said, "Speak when you are angry and you will make the best speech you will ever … Regret."

In conclusion of this point, please remember the following.

Calmness leads to communication.
Communication leads to control.
Control leads to success.
Success leads to self-esteem.
Self-esteem leads to calmness.

It is the cycle of success that begins and ends with calmness.

It is the cycle of success that begins within you and ends within you.

Constructive Criticism

You are living in a dynamic world based on actions and reactions. It is your responsibility to drive this world to be a better place for everyone. It is your responsibility to choose how you will act and how you will react. You may choose to react by ignoring the situation and remaining silent, or you may choose to react by giving criticism. If you decide to give criticism, then you have to make sure you are giving constructive criticism for the sake of bettering the community and the world. At the same time, you need to learn to accept criticism from the community around you. It is your responsibility to decide how far you can accept criticism and make it constructive and beneficial, even if it is not.

We now agree on the concept "It all begins within you." Before we talk about how to deliver and accept constructive criticism to the world, let us talk about constructive criticism to ourselves.

In this phase, you can have a conversation with yourself. You are calm and in control, and most important, you know the CEO of your organization is your heart, your brain, your soul, or your mind. But this organization has different members like your body, your hands, your eyes, and your ears. These members are not board members or decision makers, but each one has a unique and effective job. You need to deeply appreciate each organ in your body for what it is doing. Understand that these organs, like any employee in any organization, is doing its job, and any shortage in the organs' performance will affect the whole organization. Like employees in an organization, many of these organs need a vacation once in a while. Expand this concept to appreciate every member in an organization and every living creature in this world for what it is giving to life and to the rules they are performing, no matter how big or small the rules.

Let's get back to our organization, back to you. Let us assume this scenario. Your brain requires information about a subject for research. You went to the library and got some resources, as well as some internet websites. Now you need to review these materials and extract the required information.

Your eyes are a vital member in your organization, responsible for reading all these resources and feeding it back to your brain.

What do you need to do as an organization?

1. You need to decide how many hours you will work the eyes and the brain, because you can't keep reading for excessive hours and exhaust your eyes.

2. You need to support your employees with the proper tools to help them accomplish the job—for example, reading glasses for your eyes, or contact lenses, or a screen filter for your monitor.

3. You need a work environment to help the employees finish their task without getting distracted, like good lighting to support the reading process and a comfortable chair to avoid back pain, which may disturb the reading process.

Now, let us assume that you did all of these steps to guarantee a successful process, but you didn't finish the task as required. What should you do next? It is meeting time! It is not a board meeting that you decide to have every week, and it is not a daily meeting. It is a meeting to discuss certain events and find out why you didn't finish the task.

Let us start the process of constructive criticism.

1. **The meeting tone must match the tone of your personality, and that is decided by the CEO.**

This is not the time for switching rules. This is not the phase of solving the problem. This is the phase of recognizing the problem and troubleshooting.

Let us clarify this point in more detail because it is a vital point in constructive criticism. If your heart is the CEO, then you need to start with your feelings before talking about facts. Tell yourself how important this project was to you, how your feelings are affecting your performance, and how these feelings now will help you to avoid this failure next time.

Let the whole meeting's rhythm be about feelings because this is your language, this is you. This is not the time to speak a different language; this is not the time to have a conflict within yourself.

Imagine yourself speaking four languages, but one of these languages is your native language, and you are facing a life-threatening situation. Which language you will use? You will use your native language because it is not the right time to translate between languages. It is time to evaluate the situation and define the problem, so don't create a language barrier and talk with yourself in anything other than your native language.

What if your brain is the CEO? In this case, the meeting rhythm will be data and facts more than feelings. Use the language that you understand, even if it is not the one matching the situation.

Expand this concept to the world around you. When you are giving criticism to someone, start with his or her language so he or she will understand without any barriers.

2. Define the weak points and why you failed to meet the deadline of your project.

Be honest with yourself. Define the reasons, the facts, the feelings, and all the symptoms. This procedure will lead you to the employee or process that caused the failure.

Let us apply this step on our scenario. Why didn't you finish this project?

- The time was not enough.
- I couldn't read all the resources, even with enough time, because I got tired.
- I couldn't process the information from the resources.
- I was distracted by friends' problem and some family issues.

Each of these reasons will take us on a different path. That is why we need to be honest and clear about the reasons for failure.

3. Relate each of these reasons to a physical organ in your body.

Each reason may be related to more than one organ. State all the organs you think are related to the failure reasons. Let us work on each reason and see where it will take us.

- **The time was not enough.**

This reason is related to the brain because the brain is the one who initiates the project and should plan enough time. Let us ask the brain about his reasons and why he didn't plan enough time for this project.

The brain may say, "I was pushed by the heart because she was so excited about this project. I was pushed by the mind because he had some backgrounds and thoughts about this project. I was pushed by the soul because she believes we can do the project no matter the time remaining."

Things are now more clear: your problem was the communication between your board members, which means you don't have enough periodic meetings, and you don't have harmony among your heart, mind, brain, and soul, or at least between two of them.

What is your action plan?

1. Being more rational when it comes to planning time.

2. Having more periodic meetings with the board members. That can be more meditation, more time with yourself, making sure about your personality type, reviewing your thoughts and beliefs, and seeing how they match with given data and how that affects your feelings.

3. Getting ready for the second trial with all these facts and results on front of you, and feeling good about yourself because you troubleshoot the problem and resolve it.

- **I couldn't read all the resources, even with enough time, because I got tired.**

To find the responsible one for this result, we need to dig deeper and troubleshoot this symptom. What do you mean by "got tired"?

  — I feel exhausted and need more sleeping hours.

This can be a mind problem that keeps you alert and worried, which that will make you miss your sleeping hours and get tired. Or it can be a false alarm; you are getting enough sleeping hours, but you feel tired because deep inside yourself, you don't trust that you can finish this project. You don't believe in yourself, and that puts you into a vicious circle that leads you to fail the project. Be honest with yourself and define the reasons for being tired.

  — I feel pain in my back when sitting for long hours.

This is a body problem, but it's not the body responsibility. You may have a back problem, and you need to check it out; your body may need healthcare and a vacation, like any employee in an organization. Or it is as simple as having a bad chair and replacing it.

  — I get a headache every time I read.

You may need glasses, or a new monitor or screen filter. You can change the font or size of the text, or you can increase the light where you read. Find the reason behind the headache.

- **I couldn't process the information from the resources.**

Simply put, you couldn't understand what you were reading. This could be a mind problem if your mind was distracted with different issues, or you didn't choose the right resources to help you finish your project.

- **I was distracted by family issues and friends' problems.**

The good thing here is that you precisely defined the problem, and your goal is setting priorities and time management. You will not face this problem if you are setting the fifteen-minute daily meetings with board members, followed by periodic meetings every week or every month. These kinds of meetings will help you manage your time and set priorities by creating harmony between the facts, your feelings, your ideas, and your beliefs.

This is the constructive criticism technique you will need to follow with yourself every time you finish a project in your life. Either you succeeded or failed in this project; either this project was big or small. It doesn't matter. What really matters is evaluating what you did and you reached the final result.

You are troubleshooting the end results by defining your SWOT.

Strength—that is, "What did you do well in this project?"
Weakness—that is, "What did you miss and need to work on to improve?"
Opportunities—that is, "What are your chances to improve?"
Threats—that is, "What can hold you back from moving on?"

If you are able to do that with yourself, then you will be able to do it with others around you, but remember that it all starts within you.

Let us summarize this technique.

1. Choose your tone based on the person you are evaluating.

2. Divide and conquer by troubleshooting the situation, and breaking it into small modules, and then working on each module.

3. Use SWOT with every module to identify who was responsible for the failure or the success so you know what to improve next time.

Finally, "What if I am the one receiving the criticism, and it is destructive criticism?"

The answer is simple: switch this criticism around to be constructive. In any situation, you have three parameters: you, the other person, and the situation itself.

The only parameter you have full control over and full communication with is yourself. You can change only yourself, and this change will eventually spread to the other person and to the surrounding conditions. Take any criticism and switch it to be constructive. Make it a good learning opportunity, because we learn from situations and people regarding what to do and what not to do!

One of the great techniques for constructive criticism is called the sandwich technique. Always start with a good part, the area of strength and the pros. Then go to the area that you need to develop. Finally, finish with another area of strength. Simply put, you start and end with positive thoughts, and in between you evaluate the weak points. That is why it is called sandwich technique. If someone gave you destructive criticism, then be smart and make a sandwich out of it!

Communicate with yourself, and you will communicate with the whole world.

Kids

I F I WERE to choose one point out of our nine-point strategy, I would choose this point, Kids. This point sums up every point we've talked about and every point we will talk about.

Before we start talking about this point, I need you to do the following. Close your eyes for a minute and imagine this world without kids. Imagine how this world would look like and the consequences. P. D. James imagined the same situation in his novel *The Children of Men*, which became a movie of the same name. Regardless of whether or not you choose to have kids, the world without kids is a world of chaos, a world of hopelessness, a world that's lost its reason to survive, a world that's lost its purity.

If the world needs kids to sustain it, then you need also kids in your life to sustain you, to have hope, and to survive. But what if I don't have kids? You don't need to have kids. What you need is to learn from kids. What you need is to go back to when you used to be a kid—and then be that kid again!

Let us see what we can learn from kids. Let us see what we can learn from ourselves, but when we were kids. First, let us see how kids persuade all the points we've covered so far.

- **Crying**

Ask any parent to describe kids in one word, and most of them will say, "Crying." Kids are using this tool very well not just to release stress but also to communicate and to control. Some kids exploit the situation and overuse this natural gift, but these are exceptions.

As we said, crying is a way of communication, but it also helps kids to release stressful emotions and have good mental health. That is one of the reasons we are not facing depression as a common problem among kids, especially from newborn to kindergarten. When we face this problem with a kid, we will notice that his nature of crying is misused, either used too much or not used at all. This is not a result of depression, but it could be one of the reasons for depression.

Now, looking to the adult world, we will find depression is a common problem because in certain phases of our lives, we mistakenly learned to hide our tears. We are crying on the inside and acting normal on the outside until we can't handle it anymore, and then comes the depression.

The first lesson learned from kids: cry.

- **Healthy**

In this point, we talked about healthy thoughts and how it is important to drop bad ideas, bad thoughts, and bad people from your life, or at least don't let them control your mode, which will let them control your attitude. We also talked about flexibility in your thoughts.

Don't you think that kids are role models in this point? How many kids have you met who are willingly dealing with other kids whom they don't like and playing with them? How many times have you heard a kid say to another, "I don't want to play with you"?

Kids' ways of expressing their feelings may look wrong for us as adults, but as a majority, kids don't deal with people they don't like. Kids are very flexible in their thoughts, and they're fast to learn new things and new concepts because they don't have taboos. It's not until we adults start to seed taboo ideas in their minds!

How fast can they learn new languages? How fast do kids' behaviors change when they start school? Regardless of changing in the right or the wrong direction, kids are very flexible until we adults interfere in their world and change this great habit by turning them into us.

The second lesson learned from kids: be healthy and flexible.

• **Education**

Kids are like a sponge, and they use all their senses to learn about everything and get all the information they need. How many *why* and *how* questions do you hear from kids every day? How many kids hesitate or feel shy when they ask these questions?

Our nature is to ask questions and learn. Our nature is to brainstorm and throw out ideas. We grow up and forget that there are no stupid questions, but there are stupid answers. When we face these stupid answers—like

"Not now" or "Seriously? You don't know?" or "You're too young for these questions"—only then do we learn to not ask, and we start losing this natural gift of thirst to knowledge.

Every progress, every invention, and every discovery started with "Why?" If the "Why?" question itself is an invention, then I will give the patent to kids. Kids are masters of exploring, and they jump from one thing to another using their ability to quickly learn, whereas with adults the story is different because adults lean more toward exploiting, focusing on details. Adults don't jump between products like kids. Surprisingly, most successful inventions came from exploring, not exploiting. To be more specific, most successful inventions came by chance, but this chance wouldn't lead to this specific invention without the flexibility of exploring, without the ability to switch the focus on a totally different subject, without the natural gift in kids—the gift of exploring!

For example, in 1945 Percy Spencer, a communication engineer, invented the idea of a microwave device that is now a common appliance in most kitchens, simply because he noticed a piece of chocolate melted in his pocket when he was standing next to a microwave source called a magnetron. because Percy had this gift of exploring, and he noticed that the room temperature was normal and would not melt the chocolate, so he started his experiments on microwaves, and that lead us to the microwave appliance!

Another example is Wilhelm Rontgen and his discovery of the x-ray, which was pure chance. He was covering a cathode ray tube and noticed a light still glowing through the cover. The flexibility to switch thinking to a different subject led humanity to one of the greatest inventions!

The same concept of exploring can be applied to the world of business. We see companies like Microsoft, which makes only 9 percent profit from its famous product, Windows. The rest of the profit comes from new products like Azure.

There are countless examples of the benefits of exploring, using the natural gift of being a kid, asking questions, and finding answers. Of course, you need to find a balance point between exploring and exploiting, but the habit of exploring will lead you to where you need to exploit!

The third lesson learned from kids: the habit of asking questions.

- **Communication**

Kids are the masters of communication. They use all their senses to communicate with everything and everyone; they communicate with people, animals, and toys. But most important, they communicate with themselves!

Grow up, but don't get old. Keep flexible thoughts and bright ideas. Keep watching cartoons and reading comic books. Keep dreaming. Keep the grit. Keep the belief that you can achieve any goal and any dream!

You may say, "But what if I've lost it with all life's stress, work, family, and responsibilities?" Then you need someone to bring it back to you. You need a kid!

This kid could be one of your friends who didn't forget how to be a kid, or it could be your kid or a cousin, niece, or nephew. Enjoy the journey with them, and you will find the kid inside you. Only then will you open the portal for unlimited opportunities of success.

From now on, whatever you are going to do, do it with the spirit and confidence of a five-year-old kid in a superhero custom.

Meditation

I KNOW YOU SAW this coming. We will discuss this point from three different perspectives.

Meditation as a concept
Meditation as a process
Meditation as a result

Meditation as a Concept

I would like to define it as the bird view. One of the tactics to work on solving any problem is to look at the problem using the bird view! Fly away from the problem. Escape the boundaries that surround you when you are in the middle of this problem. Only then will you see different perspectives, different solutions, or different threats. But in all cases, you will see different ways to solve the problem, or you may see the problem as an opportunity. This flying away is meditation!

When you meditate, you fly away from your body, from your daily routine, and from all the activities surrounding you—those activities that once were fun but now are burdens!

As an ancient Chinese proverb said, "You need ten minutes to mediate every day, if you can't find these ten minutes, then you need one hour to mediate every day." Your need for meditation is proportional with how busy you are. Now, consider this concept of meditation and answer the following question: Who is the role model in meditation?

Yes, the answer is a kid. Being a kid is the way and the goal! If meditation is flying away from all restraints and obstacles, then kids, who are always dreaming and living in imaginary worlds, are the masters of meditation!

Meditation as a concept is very deep, and we can see it from many different aspects, but this is the angle we want to focus on. Meditation means to fly away. Look at yourself from a bird's angle and see yourself from outside. Only then will you understand more about yourself. You will see your strengths and weaknesses and define them from different aspects, which is a necessity for deciding your strategy in the game of life.

Meditation as a Process

Meditation is a decision. You can practice all the forms of meditations based on what you believe, but you still are not meditating!

Let us try to visualize this. All the day's obstacles, issues, and activities; your workload, your study, and everything you need to escape from; and everything you need to look at from different angles—these are like the earth's gravity. Now, think of yourself as a rocket that needs to escape this gravity and fly away! Could you just let that rocket fly like a plane, or do you need to give this rocket a push to escape gravity?

This push is your decision to meditate. No one can do that for you; no one can push you to meditate. People can spend hours talking to you about the benefits of meditation. Then, even if you follow all the steps, if you don't visualize it and you don't see yourself doing it, you don't take the decision to do it. You are not meditating until you decide to meditate!

Here's an example. Praying is a form of meditation, but going to the temple, the church, or the masjid, or staying home and praying, is not an actual prayer or meditation until you make the decision of complete submission to whom you're praying to. Give it a try, no matter your beliefs. Try to pray for five minutes with complete submission, forgetting the world around you. Compare your feelings and energy after this prayer to your feelings and energy after practicing the prayer as a habit.

As another example, hiking could be a form of meditation. However, you can hike for hours without meditating for even a second, if you didn't free your mind from all the thoughts that are attaching you to your daily routine and the things you need to take care later.

This point needs to be clear before we move on: meditation as a process has many different shapes based on your personality, your beliefs, and things you like to do. No matter what type of person you are, you always can find a process of meditation that suits you.

Watching a movie could be a meditation. Listing to music could be a meditation. Reading a book could be a meditation. Having a cup of coffee or tea could be a meditation. Praying, working out, yoga—these are all forms of meditation, but only if you make that decision.

Usually, meditation is related to sports, especially martial arts. And yes, martial arts can be a meditation process!

One of the famous martial arts schools that focuses on meditation as the core of its sport is kung fu. Kung fu means "skills and effort." That is how I like to see meditation!

Meditation is a skill that you will gain if you decide to put forth the effort. The effort here is the decision!

Meditation as a Result

"Why do I need to meditate?" you ask. I am sure you already saw and read a lot of articles and ads about meditation stating how it is important to meditate because it will improve your quality of life. Together, we will get deeper on talking about meditation results and what is meant by improving quality of life.

The ultimate result of meditation is to find your centroid. At the beginning of every year, the most common question among friends and families is, "What is your resolution for the new year?"

One of the common answers to this question is, "I want to find my balance." The balance point is the centroid. In any geometrical shape like a triangle, rectangle, or square, there is only one point that will keep this shape in balance This point is called the centroid.

How is that related to meditation? If you are in balance, that means you are in control of the situation. That is the ultimate goal of meditation: to always feel you are in the driver's seat. You are the action, not the reaction!

"But how will meditation help me find my balance point?"

Back to geometry. Let us take the triangle as an example. The triangle centroid is the intersection of the three medians. Three lines intersect in one point, and this point is the centroid. If you studied this geometry rule at school, then you know about the centroid. If you didn't, then you can try this fun experiment. Make the shape of triangle from any material like cardboard. Then draw a line from each vertex to the midpoint on the opposite side of the triangle. The three lines will meet at one point, and that is the centroid. Put your finger on this point, and you will find the triangle shape stays in balance on your fingertip!

You also can find your own centroid from the intersection of three lines.

1. The vertical line between you and the higher power.

No matter the name you call this higher power—God, Jesus, Allah—what really matters is the level of trust and submission you have to it. Have you seen a parent playing with his kid and throwing her in the air before catching her again? You will see this kid laughing and super happy, because this kid is 100 percent sure that her dad will catch her before she falls. That is the level of trust you need to have with this higher power: a trust that you are never alone, a trust that at the end, everything is okay (and if it is not okay, then it is not the end). The trust will keep you calm and in control because even if you are falling down, you know that the higher power will catch you before you hit the ground.

Here's another learning lesson from kids. Once there was a plane about to crash, and all the passengers were panicked except one kid. He was calm and smiling. After the plane landed safely, they asked him, "How come you were that calm?"

He said, "My dad is the pilot. I knew he would land the plane safely."

Again, that is the level of trust you need to have. Practice this level of trust, and that will be the first line for finding your centroid!

2. **The horizontal line between you and the people around you.**

This includes people like friends and family. There is no much to say here. Simply, be the change you want to see. If you want happiness from them, then be a source of happiness for them. If you want caring from them, then start caring about them. Feel strong by gaining friends, not stuff. Feel strong by letting go of small things. Feel strong by ignoring what is upsetting you. Focus on what makes you happy. Dealing with people is an art, but it doesn't require an artist—it requires a decision to be happy no matter what. Make the decision to give a little extra.

How would you feel if you went to buy a coffee, and the coffee shop gave you an extra cookie? Or say you asked someone for a survey, and she gave you extra credit? You would feel happy. Therefore give people the same feeling. Give people a little extra.

If you say thank-you to someone, add the little extra and smile. If you ask someone, "How are you doing?" add the little extra and make eye contact. If you leave a tip, always add a little extra. Always give the cookie with the coffee, and that is the second line for finding your centroid.

3. The vertical line between you and whoever needs you.

In this phase, you play God mode. In this phase, you are the shelter, and you are the source of trust to whoever needs you. This person could be a kid or a pet, or it could be someone you are mentoring at work or at school.

When you make people feel safe, you will feel safe; when you make people feel secure, you will feel secure!

A friend who always brings food and water to birds once said, "I thought I was doing these birds a favor by feeding them, but no. These birds are doing me the favor by accepting my help!"

The person you help will get this help anyway, whether from you or from someone else. Be part of the process, and be thankful that you can help. That will be the third line to finding your centroid.

With these three lines intersecting, you will find your balance. You will find your centroid!

Let us play devil's advocate. "Everything you said about meditation and centroid and balance is theoretically right, but I don't see how effective that will be in the game of life. How will it improve the quality of my life?"

To answer your concerns, I will need to tell you a story—actually, a few stories. Go get your favorite drink, and let us enjoy reading these stories. Hopefully at the end, you will see the results of meditation as your centroid.

Let us go back in time more than 1,400 years. A very wise man named Ali Ben Abo Taleb was a direct cousin of the Prophet Mohamed, the prophet of Muslims. Once, people asked Ali, "What is the strongest creature on Earth?" This was his answer.

Iron ... But wait, fire melts iron, then

Fire ... But wait, water puts down fire, then

Water ... But wait, clouds carry water, then

Clouds ... But wait, wind moves clouds, then

Wind ... But wait, mountains stop wind, then

Mountains ... But wait, man climbs mountains, then

Man ... But wait, man falls asleep, then

Sleeping ... But wait, panic takes away sleeping, then

Panic ... But wait, your mind can contain panic and control it, then

Your mind is the strongest thing on Earth!

He knew from the beginning that the answer was the mind, but he built logic to convince people who lived in the desert more than 1,400 years ago!

Now, let us fast-forward and meet Air Force Colonel George Hall, who was captured during the Vietnam War and remained a prisoner for seven years in a wooden box. In order to avoid losing his mind during this horrible experience that could drive anyone crazy, George decided to play a full game of golf every day—in his mind!

He was not imagining the whole picture of the game. He was not imagining himself playing in the future. He was playing the game in his mind as it was happening, as it was in that moment, with all the small details: every swing, every shot, and every applause. He kept doing that for seven years. Then just one week after he was released in 1973, he entered Greater New Orleans Open and shot a 76!

Let us Leave Colonel George Hall and Meet Arnold Schwarzenegger. When a reporter asked Mr. Schwarzenegger how he won the Mr. Olympia contest seven times, he didn't talk about his workout routine, and he didn't talk about his nutrition and diet system. He said, "I saw myself there. I visualized myself there. Mind over matter."

Let us now go to the Olympics in 1980, when Russians were testing a concept called visualization—how to train your mind to visualize your success. The experiment was to divide the Russian team into four groups.

Group A, with 100 percent physical training

Group B, with 75 percent physical training and 25 percent mental training

Group C, with 50 percent physical training and 50 percent mental training

Group D, with 25 percent physical training and 75 percent mental training

The results were astonishing because Group D was the best during the Olympics!

One last story before we go to the conclusion, but this time the story is personal. I am a field service engineer who's worked on troubleshooting medical equipment for more than twenty years. When I started my career, a very close friend named Almahdy Altonsy gave me advice that I live with today. He said that 60 percent of the success in this job was mind-set, and the other 40 percent was different parameters like knowledge, education, experience, and troubleshooting skills. He continued. "It is a subconscious process that every time you go for a job, you are not thinking whether or not you will fix the system. The question is how you are going to fix it, and how long it will take. You already made the decision that this problem will be fixed. You're already 60 percent on your way to success before you even start. This mind-set will grant you full access to the other 40 percent, which is your knowledge and troubleshooting skills."

On average, let us say I am doing five troubleshooting projects per week. Over twenty years, that is 4,800 service calls. Do you know how many times I failed to fix the system? Only once! That is a success rate of 99.98 percent, and that is not because of my level of knowledge or my troubleshooting skills. It was the mind-set, It was the decision to succeed that led to my success!

What is the secret? Albert Einstein said, "Imagination is more important than knowledge. For knowledge is limited, whereas imagination embraces the entire world, stimulating progress, giving birth to evolution."

Napoleon Hill, in his book *Think and Grow Rich*, said, "Whatever your mind can believe and conceive, it can achieve."

Perhaps the best way to answer this question is what Srinivasan Pillay, a Harvard MD and the author of *Leaders*, says about how visualization works: "We stimulate the same brain regions when we visualize an action as we do when we actually perform that same action." That means your brain, as a tool receiving information, cannot tell the difference between reality and imagination!

Again: your brain, as a tool receiving information, cannot tell the difference between information received by senses like sight and hearing, and information received by imagination!

When your brain receives positive information and good news, whether by physical senses or by the imagination, it will stimulate dopamine in your body. Dopamine will increase your level of happiness, satisfaction, and awareness, which will make you see hidden possibilities and different ways to achieve your goal.

Success doesn't lead to happiness. Happiness leads to success!

When you're happy, you will think positively. Imagine positive things that your mind will receive and increase the level of dopamine, which will make you more happy, more positive, and more successful! That is why we say "happy-go-lucky." Happy doesn't go lucky. Happy sees the opportunities that we don't see.

Now, be careful because your brain will work the same way in the opposite direction, when it receives negative information: instead of being happy, you will go to the vicious circle!

It all starts within you. It all starts with how you set your mind. It all starts with how you want to use your brain. Your brain is a tool like a knife. Are you going to use it to cut a fruit and enjoy eating it, or will you cut yourself?

As Laozi, an ancient Chinese philosopher and writer, said,

Watch your thoughts, they become your words
Watch your words, they become your actions
Watch your actions, they become your habits
Watch your habits, they become your character
Watch your character, it becomes your destiny.

How do we watch our thoughts? By controlling them! How do control them? By controlling our brains! How we control our brains? By controlling our minds!

Your mind is "the strongest creature ever created." Your mind could be your best friend and your ultimate power, or it could be your worst undefeated enemy. Your mind and the thoughts in it will shape your destiny.

That is why we need meditation, that is why we need to find our inner peace within our minds, and that is why we need to help our minds find their centroid. That is why we need to back up our dreams with faith, with the belief that we can achieve our dreams no matter what.

We must train our minds to worry about what we can control and stop worrying about what we can't control.

One of the guiding rules that I make sure to repeat to my kids is the PP rule. Of course, that brought a lot of laughter when pronouncing the letters. PP here stands for "practice and pray." With these two Ps, you will get what you are looking for. Practice so you gain full control of your tools, like knowledge and skills. Pray so you master controlling your mind and see where you need to drive your practice.

As mentioned at the beginning of this point, prayer is a kind of meditation. That is why we need meditation!

Acceptance

O NE OF THE most important tools that will help you achieve your goals is acceptance: accepting your failure, accepting your weakness, accepting different points of view on all aspects, accepting that people may not accept you, and accepting what you don't agree with. This is a good start to seeing the difference between accepting and agreeing.

If, for any political or religious reasons, your agreement bandwidth is limited to a certain extent, then your bandwidth of acceptance as a human should be wider to include every thought and belief. Accept what you don't agree with!

To easily understand this point, we need to talk about the term "fuzzy logic," and what it is doing with the concept of acceptance. Let us go back to 1965 and meet Professor Lotfi A. Zadeh, a mathematician, computer scientist, electrical engineer, artificial intelligence researcher, and professor emeritus of computer science at the University of California, Berkeley. Professor Zadeh was working on a project to make computers understand common language terms.

Computers were devices based on binary language, and they could understand only ones and zeros, voltage or no voltage. That made them very fast and very accurate, but they couldn't make decisions and can't control systems. Remember, we are talking about 1965.

For example, at that time, a computer could understand the term "hot" as a one, and the term "cold" as a zero. But what about "warm," "cool," and "moderate"? That was why in 1965, Zadeh started working on the theory of fuzzy sets, and in 1973 he proposed the theory of fuzzy logic.

Simply put, fuzzy logic creates degrees of probabilities between the two extreme cases of one and zero. Wait, what?

Think of fuzzy logic as a positive, energetic person who always meditates, as a person who found her centroid and controls her mind, as a person who's always looking for positivity and is always looking for the ones, not for zeros. She always sees the good part in anything and then accepts this thing and describes it with that good part.

Back to our example about hot and cold. If hot is one, then warm will be 0.75 hot, and moderate will be 0.5 hot. We keep going until we reach the other extreme, cold. Based on fuzzy logic, it will not be zero but 0.001 hot.

So simply put, there is no zero—we always relate things to one, and we always describe things referring to one.

Let us take another example to make fuzzy logic clearer. Before fuzzy logic, computers as devices based on the binary system would understand genius as one and stupid as zero. After fuzzy logic, computers were still devices based on the binary system; that didn't change. They would understand

genius as 1.0,

brilliant as 0.75 genius,

creative as 0.6 genius,

knowledgeable as 0.4 genius,

and so on until we reach to the other extreme, which was stupid. However, stupid will not be zero but 0.05 genius.

The probabilities between the different stages will vary based on the project, the programmer, and the context of the experiment, but the concept would stay the same.

Fuzzy logic will define the best-case scenario stage as one and then accept every other stage with a degree of probability referring to this absolute one. Even the extreme worst-case scenario stage that is completely opposite to the one will still have a degree of probability in relation to one.

Fuzzy logic was the core of many computer science fields like neural networks, artificial intelligence, control systems, and machine learning.

While we taught computers to move from binary logic to fuzzy logic, we humans moved back to binary logic! We started doing everything very fast and very accurate, but we lost control. We started to look at ourselves and the world around us as ones and zeros, forgetting that in this life, there is no absolute one or absolute zero!

We forgot there are a lot of probabilities between good and bad. We forgot that in every good, there is a probability of bad, and in every bad, there is a probability of good. Then we became prejudiced and pointed to things as either good or bad, either right or wrong, either one or zero.

For example, say that you are entrepreneur, have your own business, and are hiring. There is a person who is dedicated to the job, goal oriented, intelligent, diplomatic, and tactful. Now, if that is all that you know about this person, would you consider this person as a candidate with some potential and give him an interview? I think the answer is yes! Why? Because this person has some potential and skills that you would like to use in your firm.

Maybe you're not yet sure if this person is a fit for the job, but you would give him a chance for an interview because he has some potential and skills.

Allow me to introduce you to that person. This person is … the devil.

Yes, Satan is dedicated, goal oriented, intelligent, and tactful. But we never look to those characteristics because we consider Satan as the absolute zero.

On the other hand, you will find that people appreciate these characteristics in Satan and ignore that he is a vicious deceiver and seducer. They may consider him the absolute one.

Both groups are wrong! In this system, there are no absolute zeros or absolute ones. The only exception of this rule is God himself because he is the absolute one. God is not within the system—God created the system, and that makes perfect sense because absolute zero can't come from absolute one. God has his touch on everything, and for that, everything in this system has part of the one, but with different probabilities.

That is why every creature in this system is a fraction of one, even the extreme case of evil, the devil himself. Satan is a fraction of one, a fraction of good characteristics. Yes, a very small fraction, but it is still there!

You may say, "But what if I don't believe in God? How I can apply the same concept of fuzzy logic?"

Let us speak science. In physics, there is no clear definition of darkness, because darkness is defined as the absence of light. Now, when you go to a very dark room where you can't see anything, after some time your eyes will start to adapt to the amount of light that was already in the room since the beginning. Your eyes accept this amount of light and adjust to be able to see by using this small fraction of light. Therefore the room was not dark from the beginning; your eyes refused to accept this amount of light, but when that changed, you started to see.

Let me emphasize that again: the same amount of light was there when you thought it was complete darkness. Only when your eyes accepted this amount of light did you start to see! In any darkness, there is light;

you simply need the time to accept that amount of light to be able to see.

In any bad situation, there is a gift; you simply need to accept the situation to see the gift. Within any person, there is good and bad. You must accept the person to see the good part and understand the part you called bad, because at the end it may not be that bad!

Teach yourself to think like fuzzy logic and test yourself every once in a while, whenever you are in a conversation with someone, or you're reading a book or watching a movie. If you find yourself asking, "What is the point?" or you're trying to reach conclusions based on your beliefs and previous experiences before finishing and taking your time to think about the given data and evidence, then you are still looking for a point for one final result. You're still looking for yes or no, for ones or zeros; you're still thinking binary. But if you find yourself saying, "What did I like about this book, or this movie, or this conversation?" or, "I will not have a conclusion until I analyze all the given data," or, "What else could be there? I didn't see it," only then you are thinking with fuzzy logic. You are looking for the one, or the fractions of the one, and only then you are you part of the fuzzy logic world! Welcome to the world of accepting others' personalities, beliefs, and thoughts!

If you still confused, let us have a fun experiment. Let us read the following story and try to think about it from a fuzzy logic perspective!

Our story is about Sarah, a very energetic, thirty-five-year-old woman. She was tall, blonde, and athletic, and she worked in human resources with one of the big firms in California. Sarah was single and lived alone in her house in a suburb close to Los Angeles.

Sarah started her day early in morning jogging on a trail near her house. No matter whether it was hot or cold, sunny or rainy, she always started her day with running.

One day, it was a cold, unlike most of the days in Los Angeles. Rain started with a very dim light, like the sun refused to wake up that morning. Sarah was jogging on the trail, and then she suddenly stopped. The dim light from the sun reflected on something, on one of the corners. There was something bright and huge, and the water dripping with the light reflections made this thing look brighter and beautiful.

Sarah carefully came closer to this thing only to see it moving very slowly, trying to hide from the rain and the cold. It was a huge, bright orange snake!

Sarah whispered to herself, "I've never seen a beautiful, huge snake like this."

While she looked at the snake and thought about what to do, something happened: they made eye contact. It was at this moment that their eyes met, and she realized in this moment that she couldn't leave him alone. She felt pity and made the decision that this snake was going to be her pet! Sarah managed to take the snake with her back home.

At home, she fed him and kept him warm. Now she had a new friend!

Two months passed, and the snake lived with Sarah, always making eye contact with her and always following her everywhere. No matter what she was doing, when she turned around, she found him looking to her. At night when she went to bed, he got into bed with her and slithered around her, seeking warmth and safety!

One day, the snake stopped eating or drinking, Sarah tried everything, such as different foods and drinks, but he refused to eat or drink anything. He still looked to her all the time, and he still went to bed every night seeking warmth by wrapping himself around her, but he would not take food or drink.

After a few days, Sarah got worried about her pet and decided to make a visit to the vet. At the clinic, the vet checked the snake and then talked to Sarah.

Tell me, Sarah, how long you have this snake?"

Sarah replied, "More than two months. Tell me, is he sick? Is it bad?"

"Okay, Sarah. Before I tell you what is going on with your snake I need to know his habits at home during these two months."

Sarah told the vet everything she'd noticed about the snake. The vet nodded his head and listened to her. At the end, the vet looked to Sarah and said, "Sarah, listen to me carefully. Your pet stopped eating and drinking not because he is sick, but because he is getting ready to eat you!"

Sarah looked at him with shock, and the Vet continued.

"He is looking at you all the time not because he misses you, but because he is measuring you with his eyes! When he goes with you to the bed and wraps himself around you, he's not seeking warmth. He is checking your size to see how long he needs to wait before the right moment. Your pet is getting ready for a big meal—you!"

Without saying a word, Sarah took her snake and left the clinic.

A few days later, two of Sarah's friends were talking and wondering where Sarah was and why she was not answering her phone. They tried to call her one more time, but she never answered.

Now, let us see whether we are able to process this fictional story using the fuzzy logic concept. I will ask you a few questions, and we will see how to answer them with a fuzzy logic concept and with a binary logic concept.

1. **What happened to Sarah?**
- The snake ate Sarah. (binary)
- I don't know all options on the table. She may have lost her phone, or she is sad because she got rid of the snake, or she doesn't want to talk to these friends—or the snake ate her! (fuzzy)

2. **Should Sarah trust the vet?**
- Yes. He is an expert. (binary)
- Well, she had to consider his opinion because he is an expert, but at the same time she had to consult more than one vet and do some research. (fuzzy)

3. **Why did the snake stopped eating?**
- The snake was getting ready to eat Sarah. (binary)

- Many options are on the table. The snake might be getting ready for a big meal, or the snake was sick, or it was his season to hibernate. (fuzzy)

4. **Did the story reflect some thoughts and ideologies that you believe?**
- Yes, and I looked to the story based on that. For example, the story is like immigration issues and crossing borders, That is how I saw the story characters. (binary)
- Yes, this is normal. Any story will reflect on us based on beliefs and personal experiences. However, I didn't let that affect my opinion or being prejudice! (fuzzy)

5. **If the pet in the story was any other animal, would you see the story in a different way?**
- Yes. I don't like snakes, and that was part of my conclusion about the story. Or, I like snakes, and that affected how I saw the story. (binary)
- No. Regardless of my feelings about having a snake as a pet, I put that aside when I listened to the story, and my conclusion was based on facts and data. (fuzzy)

I hope this example will help you to switch your thinking approach from binary (black and white, right and wrong) to fuzzy logic, where all possibilities on the table!

We need to understand that acceptance is not about giving up our beliefs and thoughts. It is about understanding that our beliefs are not 100 percent right and others' beliefs are not 100 percent wrong, because there is nothing 100 percent right or wrong. Following this concept will create a common ground between your thoughts and others thoughts, which will create an area of understanding. From this area, we will accept what we don't agree, and we will agree to disagree!

Now, let us see how that concept of acceptance will help us to successfully survive and enjoy the game of life.

When you start to accept your faults and your mistakes, when you start to accept others' beliefs and concepts, and when you sincerely accept that nothing and no one is 100 percent right or wrong, then you are applying the main concept of diversity, and diversity is the core of acceptance. Diversity is not about agreeing with the other person's differences, but it is about accepting other person's differences and going through it until together you find a common area of agreement. Only then will you start to believe and live with this quote that I mentioned earlier.

You are better than anyone who walked on the earth in something, and anyone who has walked on the earth is better than you in something.

Only then will you defeat the mother of all bad ideas. Wait, what? Is there such a thing as the mother of all bad ideas? Yes.

This is good news because once we know it, and once we know how to deal with it, then we're welcome to a world without bad ideas!

The bad news is that every time life distracts us, we start to fall in the trap of the mother of bad ideas. Then we start giving it different names like pride, dignity, and honor. It is very important to emphasize that there is nothing wrong with these characteristics; we all agree that these are very respected and important characteristics that we should keep and work on improving in ourselves. What is wrong is falling into the trap under the name of these characteristics, the trap of the mother of all bad ideas, also known as...**EGO.**

Do you like history?

History shows us how ego is the source of all bad ideas—and how acceptance will save us from this trap.

Let us go back in time. Let us go back even before time. Let us meet Adam, Eve, and Satan. All holy books agree on the story of Adam, Eve, and Satan. There are some minor differences and different versions, but the core of the story is the same among all religions.

The story says when God created Adam, he ordered all angels to bow to Adam as a sign of respect to God's creation. They all did so except Satan, who refused to bow.

We all know why Satan refused to bow, and how he confronted God by claiming that he was created from fire and so was better than Adam, who was created from clay. We all know what stopped Satan from obeying a direct order from God: ego.

And that is how it all began: an endless war between Satan and Adam, a war started thousands of years ago that will keep going until the end of days, a war started by ego.

We also know that Adam and Eve themselves disobeyed God's order and ate from a tree. So why did God forgive Adam and Eve and give them and the rest of humanity a second chance, but he didn't do the same with Satan? It's because Adam and Eve admitted their mistake and asked for forgiveness, whereas Satan didn't. Something stopped him from apologizing and asking for forgiveness—something called ego.

Not everyone agrees with this version of the story, but no matter what version you believe, you will still find ego as the source of all bad ideas. For those who don't believe this story, don't worry; we have more stories to prove to you how ego is the source of all bad ideas!

Now that we are on Earth, let us see what ego did to us, but this time let us speak science! This time we will go back to the fourth century BC, between 384 and 322 BC, to meet one of the greatest ancient Greek philosophers and scientists. He was also the private tutor of Alexander the Great. Let us meet Aristotle!

Aristotle had a theory that Earth was the center of the universe, and everything else like the sun, the stars, and the other planets revolved around it. This theory survived for more than two thousand years.

In AD 1633, an Italian physicist and astronomer, Galileo Galilei, was convicted of heresy by the Church for his belief that Earth was not the center of the universe and, like any other planet, revolved around the sun. Galileo Galilei spent rest of his life under house arrest.

After three hundred years, the Church admitted that he was right!

Why did the theory of Earth as the center of the universe survive all that time? Because it matched our ego. We were the center of universe, and everything else revolved around us. Regardless of all the scientific facts presented by Galileo Galilei (and before him, Nicolaus Copernicus), we preferred to live in an illusion that matched our ego rather than face the truth that would help us move forward. Again, ego is the mother of all bad ideas.

Let us leave science and talk about something else. Let us talk about religions. All these conflicts between different religions, whether subtle conflicts or clear disputes, rage, anger, and death! Radicals from any religion believe that only they deserve to live, and only they are going to heaven!

The fact is that all religions and beliefs share more than 90 percent of their thoughts and beliefs. We can live with this 90 percent, and we can even live together with much less than 90 percent—but only when we let go of ego and accept each other!

It is ego that makes us forget that religion is a language. It doesn't matter what language you speak, but the message you deliver is what matters. We all try to deliver the same message, but again, ego makes us focus on the language, not the message!

We can keep going with all different subjects in life—history, science, art, religion, and politics—and we will always find that the mother of any problem can be traced to ego.

Now, what if we look to ourselves? Ego is what's stopping us from learning and improving. Ego is what's stopping us from trying new things in life.

How? Your fear of losing is mainly driven by your ego. Think of it from this perspective. You don't want to try new things because you don't want your image in front of people to look bad. Your ego tries to keep you in a comfort zone where you feel good about yourself and where you believe other people feel good about you.

Finally, ego will come to you in many different shapes, and you are the only one who can tell whether it is pride, dignity, or ego. That is why you need to be careful when you are fighting with your ego and trying to manage it. You don't need to manage your pride, your dignity, your personality, or your self-confidence because there is a silver lining between all these good characteristics and ego.

The key here is to keep the balance in this quote.

You are better than any person who's walked on this earth in something, and any person who's walked on this earth is better than you in something.

The first part will help you keep your self-confidence; the second part will stop self-confidence from turning into something ugly. The first part will make you wake up every morning happy; the second part will make you wake up every morning anxious to learn new things. The first part will help you facing other people's egos with a confident smile that you are better than this person in something; the second part will help you fight your ego with a modest, humble smile. Life is about keeping yourself in balance between the two parts of this quote.

Back to our point of acceptance. Now we understand the importance of it and how ego will try to stop us from accepting what we don't agree with! Let me ask a question.

I put down my ego, I learned to accept others, and most important I accepted myself, my faults, and my problems. How would that help me succeed if I accepted my faults and weak points and live with them?

When you accept your faults, that doesn't mean you live with them. It means you mastered the first step of fixing these faults, because the first step to solving a problem is to recognize this problem! If you identify the problem and didn't accept it, you will be alert and worried all the time, and this is when other mistakes will happen.

But when you accept it and start applying previous points in our CHECKMATE strategy, then you will work on a game plan to fix this fault in a way that suits you.

Before we leave this point, I want you to think again about the word *diversity* and how some people or governments see it as leverage and leading to success, whereas others see it as an obstacle and leading to chaos.

The difference here is acceptance! That is why you see countries like the United States and India with many races, ethnicities, and religions living together in harmony, whereas other countries with a majority race and minorities of other races live in chaos. If you are looking for one word to describe the difference between these two cases, it is acceptance! Be the change you want to see in this world. Let it start within you, and learn to accept.

Now, tell me your thoughts about this point. Do you agree or accept—or both?

Tactful

D O YOU SEE anything in common between devils and profits, between saints and demons, or between leaders and dictators? The answer is that both aspects are tactful. Satan is tactful, but so are Jesus, Mohammed, Buddha, and Confucius. Lincoln was tactful, but so was Hitler.

Based on the Quran, the holy book of Muslims, when God asked Moses to talk to Pharaoh of Egypt and guide him to the right path of God, Moses asked God to have his brother with him. Why? Because his brother was tactful. His brother knew how to put words together in a convincing way.

Even with the great message that Moses had to deliver, and even with God himself protecting Moses, Moses was very clever and tactful to think about the best way to deliver the message. He knew that a tactful person knew how to put the words together—and that by itself was tactful from profit Moses!

Here's another example from the Muslim world to show the importance of choosing the right tool to deliver the message. Before Muslims pray, they call for prayer using Azan, a special call for the prayer, using the same words for more than 1,400 years. Knowing the importance for this Azan to Muslims, you would assume the first one who called for the prayer using these special words would be the prophet himself. No. Prophet Mohammed picked a guy named Belal because Belal had a beautiful and strong voice.

Another example is Satan himself, the way he presented the sin to us, and how easily we may fall in his trap of nice words and tactics.

There are a countless number of examples on both the good and bad sides. No matter how great your message, no matter how many powerful tools you have or who is covering your back, being tactful is the luxury wagon that will deliver your message and guarantee that your audience will give you 100 percent in listening and attention.

But how can one be tactful? We can look at the tactful tool from these perspectives.

1. When you should speak and when you should not.

2. The tools you can use to deliver your message.

3. How to read your audience before delivering your message, and then how you adjust your message based on the audience.

Let us start with a story. Once upon a time, there was a country that used the guillotine to execute guilty criminals. Three men were going to be executed: a priest, a lawyer, and a scientist. The story didn't tell us why these men would be executed or whether it was one case or different cases, but here we were on execution day!

The crowd gathered around the guillotine, calling for blood. Most of them didn't even know why these people would be executed, but they kept shouting, excited to see heads flying in the air and blood everywhere.

The guards started with the priest and took him in front of the guillotine. Only then did the priest start shouting, "God, God, God! I believe in God, and only God is my savior." The guards put the priest's head down and released the guillotine to cut off the priest's head. Only then did a miracle happen. The blade stopped right before it touched the priest's neck.

The crowd went crazy and started shouting, "God, God, God! Release the priest!"

The guards listened to the crowd and released the priest.

Then it was the lawyer's turn. Right in front of the guillotine, the lawyer screamed, "Justice, justice! I don't believe in God as the priest, but I believe in justice, and only justice is my savior."

The same thing happened: the blade stopped right before touching the lawyer's neck. Then the whole crowd started screaming again. "Justice, justice! Release the lawyer!" The guards released the lawyer.

Now it was the scientist's turn. In front of the guillotine, the scientist look to the crowd and said, "I don't believe in God as the priest does, and I don't believe in justice as the lawyer does. But I believe in science and observations, and based on data and facts, I think there is a knot in the robe stopping the blade from going all the way down."

The guards checked the robe, and yes, they found the knot. They release the knot, and this time the crowd kept shouted as the blade went all the way down!

Tactful is not just knowing what to say, how to say it, and when to say it. It is also knowing when to stop talking and when to keep your thoughts to yourself. It is about knowing your audience and thinking for few seconds, asking yourself, "Do I really need to share this information with this audience?"

The scientist should have kept his observation to himself in order to keep his head!

The story didn't say whether the priest or the lawyer knew about the knot. For the sake of our conversation here about being tactful, let us assume they knew about it, but both of them were tactful. They used an observation to serve their goal, which was saving their lives. Then they used the right words to match their personalities. The priest used God's name because it fit him and would make the audience believe him. The lawyer simply justice because it fit better with him and gave him more credibility with the audience. In the end, they both survived—unlike the scientist, who thought that his honesty would save his life!

He failed to read his audience and for that he failed to keep his life!

You know the saying "A picture is worth a thousand words"? Using the same concept, a story is better than a thousand lectures. A story can deliver your message in a way that's more powerful than explaining a concept or detailing a theory. That was the main reason behind one of the most famous storybooks in history, *Kalila & Dimna: Fables of Bedba*. It's a book of about thirty stories in the animal world, where each story will easily deliver a message and explain a concept. The story of how this book came to life is as exciting as the stories within the book itself.

Because a story is better than a thousand lectures, and as I know you like stories, let us enjoy the story of the book *Kalila & Dimna*, and then we will see how that will help being tactful.

Our story begins with Alexander the Great marching to invade India. The king of India at that time, Fur, refused to surrender to Alexander and started preparing a huge army to face the invader. The army included all different kinds of animals: lions, jackals, wolves, and elephants.

When Alexander learned about this army, he asked his counsel to bring him all the professions in the army who joined him from all the countries he'd conquered. Alexander asked them to build copper statues of horses and knights on wheels and make them hollow. Then he filled the statues with sulfur and covered these statues to look like real knights. He put the statues at the front of the army and a lit fire under them. The copper became very hot. When the elephants attacked these statues, thinking they were attacking real knights, they got burned by the hot copper. They stumbled back and created chaos in the Indian army—a chaos that Alexander used well to achieve victory on that day!

Alexander left one of his men as the governor of India and moved on to another battle. Right after he left, the people of India rebelled and got back their country. They had a new king from their royal blood, King Debshleem. In the beginning, Debshleem was a very good king, but with time and with all that power and authority, he turned into a dictator.

During his time, there was a wise philosopher named Bedba. Bedba didn't want his name to be mentioned in the era of a dictator, so he gathered his students and shared his thoughts with them. He said, "I will go to Debshleem and advise him to be a fair and a wise king, as he used to be."

His students were frightened and advised him to not go. They said, "Debshleem is a very powerful king. He only listen to himself, and he will execute you. Then he will chase all of us, and death will be our fate!"

Bedba said, "You remind me the story of the elephant and the pigeon. Once upon a time, there was a strong elephant that used to go every day to the lake to drink water. On his way there was pigeon and her nest. One day the elephant was walking as usual, and he accidentally smashed the nest and killed all the pigeon babies.

"The mother pigeon came back to find her nest destroyed and her babies killed. She knew that the elephant had done it, but why? Angry and very sad, she went to the elephant and said, 'You destroyed my nest and killed my babies. Why did you do that?'

"Without apologizing or saying it was an accident, the elephant arrogantly replied, 'So what? How dare you talk to me like that. Go away before I smash you too!'

"The mother pigeon sadly flew away, feeling weak and helpless. She wondered how she could avenge her kids. She went to her pigeon friends and told them what had happened, adding that she wanted to avenge her kids.

"They told her the same thing you are telling me now. They said, 'But the elephant is very huge and strong. He will kill you. You should forget about him!'

"The mother pigeon couldn't forget her kids, and she couldn't overcome her feelings of injustice! A few days later, she went back to her pigeon friends and said, 'All I need from you is to fly around the elephant and distract him until I poke his eyes and avenge my kids!' It was like a magic moment as her friends sensed her pain and decided to help her.

"That morning, all the pigeons flew around the elephant, teasing and annoying him until the right moment. Then the mother pigeon flew in and poked his eyes. The plan worked, and the elephant turned blind and helpless!

"But the mother Pigeon didn't stop at this point. She went to the frogs and said, 'I want to ask you a favor. I want you to go to the cliff and start making loud noise.'

It was another magic moment as they listened to her and agreed to her plan.

"The next day, the elephant slowly walked, counting on his hearing sense as he tried to reach the lake to drink water. He followed the sound of the frogs, thinking they were gathering around the lake. A moment later, he fell down from the cliff, and before he let go his last breath, he heard the mother pigeon saying, 'Today, I avenged my kids! You underestimated my power, but today I live and you die!'"

Bedba looked to his students and said, "I will go to Debshleem, and I will talk to him, but I want you to get ready to leave the city so if the king executes me, then you can run away."

Bedba went to Debshleem and started talking about justice and how history honored great kings but had contempt for oppressive rulers. Bedba's speech was not tactful at all, and the king ordered his execution for the next day.

That night, Debshleem couldn't sleep. He thought that executing Bedba may bring a rebellion because Bedba has a lot of followers. The next day, Debshleem called Bedba and asked him to repeat his speech again—but to choose his words wisely.

This time, Bedba was calmer and talked about how Debshleem used to be a great king. History may forget all of his great work and remember only his era of injustice. This time Debshleem decided to listen to Bedba, and he ruled his kingdom with justice and fairness. He kept Bedba close to him as a counselor.

Like any good king, Debshleem started to focus on arts and books. He noticed that all his ancestors had books to represent their eras, so he asked Bedba to write a book that challenged the time—a book about which history would say, "This book was written in the era of Debshleem. It's a book full of wisdom and morals, but it's also easy to read for all people."

Bedba loved the idea and asked the king to give him one year. He locked himself in a room with one of his students for the whole year to come out with a storybook for all time. The book was *Kalila & Dimna: Fables of Bedba*.

This book was one of the sacred secrets in India until it was stolen by a Persian merchant. When the Arabs invaded Persia, they found the book and translated it into different languages, spreading it all over the world. That is why the world knows *Kalila & Dimna: Fables of Bedba*.

Storybooks are great tools that help you to be tactful. They will grab your audience's attention and make them listen to you once you say these magical words: "Once upon a time …"

In *Kalila & Dimna*, you will find stories about animals. Each story will help you deliver a concept or idea in an easy way that both kids and adults can understand.

Do you still remember the guillotine story and the lesson learned from it? You may find this story a little bit dark to explain to some of your audience because of age or culture restrictions. Let us share a story from *Kalila & Dimna* that will explain the same concept. This time, our story's characters are a tortoise and two pelicans.

Once upon a time, there was a nice lake filled with different kinds of fish. A tortoise and two some pelicans lived around the lake, and they were close friends. Life was easy, with food and water around.

During the summer season, drought started affecting the area, and the water in the lake receded. The two pelicans decided to fly to another area, where they could live around a bigger lake, but there was one problem: they didn't want to leave behind their friend the tortoise. The tortoise couldn't fly or even walk fast enough.

The tortoise had an idea. She said, "I will get a strong tree branch, and you will hold it with your feet on both sides. I will bite on that tree branch in the middle, and we will all fly to the other lake!"

The pelicans liked the idea, and the Tortoise started looking for a good strong tree branch that she could bite.

After a while, the two pelicans were flying and holding a tree branch, and the tortoise was biting on it! Everyone in the village looked to that strange view and wondered why the pelicans were carrying this tree branch—and why this tortoise was biting it!

One of the villagers said, "This is strange. What if this tortoise opens her mouth?"

Another said, "What if the pelicans let go of the tree branch?"

The tortoise listened to all of that and kept her mouth closed around the tree branch.

Then another villager said, "I think this is a stupid idea, and this tree branch will break."

Only then did the tortoise look to him, and she said, "This is a brilliant idea. It is my idea, and I picked this tree branch to hold me. My friends will never let go, and I will never open my mouth!"

That was what she was going to say, but she never said it because as soon as she opened her mouth, she fell down and dropped dead!

The tortoise in our story, like the scientist in the guillotine story, couldn't keep her mouth shut, and for that she lost her life!

You may wonder why the pelicans didn't defend the plan and talk to the villagers. The answer to this point could be in many forms.

- They didn't hear the villagers.
- They were focused on the mission.
- They didn't want to waste their energy talking.

No matter what the pelicans were thinking, it's the same as what the priest and the lawyer were thinking about. In the end, they all shared the same fate: they stayed alive! The scientist and the tortoise shared the same fate.

Being tactful is about choosing your battles. You may lose one battle, but you will win the war as long as you are tactful.

It's the same in chess. You may sacrifice an important piece, but you will be the one who saying checkmate at the end of the game, and that is what really counts!

We are not talking about letting go of your morals or beliefs. We are focusing on the situation that will pressure you to talk and prove your point, the situation that will pressure you to prove they are wrong and you are right, and the situation that will push and awaken your worst enemy, the ego.

Yes, the ego is the mother of all bad ideas, and only then you will lose your war because now you are serving your ego.

But how to deal with this kind of situation? Simply be tactful and ask yourself the following.

1. Will talking serve my goal, or should I keep silent? (The tortoise should keep silent.)
2. Do I need to mention facts that is no one else's concern? (The scientist should not have talked about the knot.)
3. If I have to talk, what should I say, and how should I say it? Who are my audience? (Well, that is another story!)

Our story this time is about a situation that requires you to talk, but how to talk and what to say is what we will learn. Our story happened in one of the prisons where guards were very tough and rude with all prisoners—all of them except one prisoner, Sam Smith. The guards were so nice to him and gave him some slack.

All prisoners thought Sam was spying on them and worked for the guards. One day, prisoners decided to talk with Sam about their doubts.

Sam listed to them then start talking. "I want to assure you I have nothing to do with the guards. However,

I see how they are treating you and how they are treating me, and I know the reason!

Tell me, when you write letters to your wives, do you talk about the guards?"

One of the prisoners said, "Yes, we do. I always tell my wife how awful and rudely the guards are treating us!" All prisoners agreed on that.

Sam looked to them and said with a smile, "In my letters, I always write good things about the guards—how nice they are, how the food is good, and how I appreciate the guards' effort. I also thank the guards all the time for their hard work and all the services they provide us!"

Prisoners looked at him very confused, and one of them said, "How are these letters related to the way the guards treat us? Why should we thank them for something they are not doing?"

Sam said, "The guards read all your letters before sending them to your families. Change what you write about them, and I am sure they will change the way they are treating you. Also, they like to be thanked. Give them that feeling, and they will appreciate it!"

Two weeks later, the guards were still treating the prisoners in a very bad way, but they also treated Sam very badly—even worse than other prisoners!

Sam was very confused and asked the prisoners, "Did you write what I told you in the letters?"

One of the prisoners said, "Yes, and we told our families that Sam Smith taught us this trick to write good things about the guards and to give them a fake smile and fake appreciation, so the bad guards will treat us better!"

Know your audience. Sam could deliver the same message but in a different way. Sometimes you need to change the way you deliver the message, not the message itself, and that is tactful! Evaluate when you should stay silent and when you should talk. Evaluate the value of your message to the audience and whether you should deliver it. Evaluate your tools and whether there is a better tool or a better person who can deliver your message in a better way—and then don't hesitate to use this tool or person!

Always keep an eye on why you need to deliver this message and what the consequences are. Only then will you be tactful!

Enjoy

Is THIS THE last point in our CHECKMATE strategy, or this was the theme and the core of all the previous points? Or is it both?

I was seven years old when I started to watch the TV show *The Incredible Hulk*. If you didn't watch this show, I highly recommend you do so! On the first episode, when Doctor David Banner started to scan himself with gamma radiation and pointed the crosshair to his forehead, I was taken away. I wondered, "What is this machine, and what can I do to be around this machine?"

That was the first step in my future career as a biomedical engineer. Years after that, I was around these x-ray machines almost every day.

I always get these compliments from my workmates about how they enjoy working with me, and I usually answer them with the same answer. I enjoy my job, because every time I am doing my job, I remember this seven-year-old kid and how he was amazed by this machine and by what it could do—or what I thought it could do.

I am still fighting this desire, every time I am around these x-ray systems, to expose myself just a little bit and become the next Hulk. Then I remind myself it will probably lead to death, not being a superhero!

I enjoy my work and that helps me move forward and create a healthy, fun environment around my workmates because I link what I am doing to good memories from the past!

Before we leave *The Incredible Hulk*, I would like to share with you a story from the show. You know that I like stories, and if you're still reading this book, you do too! This story helped me to understand and go through many situations in my life's journey.

In one of the episodes, David Banner met Caroline Fields, who was helping him in his research to find a cure. It turned out she herself had a terminal disease.

One day David looked to Caroline and said, "Would you marry him?"

Caroline looked to him. "But why, David? I am dying!"

David looked straight in the eyes and said, "I once heard this story about a man walking in a park, and suddenly he saw a lion coming closer to him. The man started running, and the lion chased him until the man reached an edge of a cliff. By the cliff, there was a tree branch. The man hung on the tree branch to jump down to the other edge of the cliff, but right before he jumped he spotted another lion waiting for him down there! The man thought to go back and climb up, but the first lion was still waiting for him! Between the lion at the top and the lion at the bottom, the man stayed hanging on the tree branch.

"Then he spotted a wild strawberry next to him. He extended his hand to the strawberry and grabbed it. He started to eat the strawberry, and for a moment he forgot the two lions and only thought about how delicious this strawberry was. You are this wild strawberry, Caroline!"

Caroline replied, "I love you, David!"

My dear reader, the end is coming anyway, either from the lion at the top or from the lion at the bottom. While you are hanging on the tree, striving to survive, don't forget about the wild strawberry. Don't forget to enjoy your life, because that what will give your life meaning and value!

I am sure most of us, if not all of us, know about the quote "Life is a journey, not a destination." But do we apply this quote all the time? Do we really understand the meaning of this quote? Do we really know that at the end of this race, we will face one of the lions, but what really matter is how we enjoyed the wild strawberry?

One of the books that I highly recommend and that will help you understand the concept of enjoying your life is *The Alchemist* by Paulo Coelho. The book is about a shepherd looking for a treasure. To find this treasure, he had to travel all over the world. I am not going to ruin the book for you, but one of the great lessons I learned from this book was the treasure in the journey. The treasures were the places he visited, the people he met, and the food he tried. If he was only focusing on the goal, he would never have found the real treasure! I am not going to say any more details about this book, though I highly recommend it. But first we need to finish what we've started here.

One of the core elements of enjoying your life is to be take risks. By this, I don't mean living your life on the edge. I mean enjoying some calculated risks in your work, in your career, and even in a game you play. Let me explain this point in more detail. I hope you enjoy this story, called "I Am Not Going to Die Tonight." I read different version of this story years ago, and I've added a few things to it so it can help explain how we should enjoy life.

The sky was so clear tonight, and the stars were so bright. He'd never seen the stars that close before, but tonight he felt he could touch them, could walk around them. Tonight, he finally felt alive.

All these thoughts ran across his mind while he lay on his back and looked to the sky with a smile on his face. His thoughts kept going, remembering the same day eighteen years ago—the day that had literally changed his life forever!

Eighteen years ago that day was his graduation day, and his birthday as well. His thoughts stopped for a second. He muttered to himself ironically, "Happy birthday to me!"

His thoughts went on again to that day when he turned twenty-two years old.

All his dreams were about to be true, and all the pains would turn to gains. His friends were celebrating his birthday tonight! A bright future was in front of his eyes, and he had one game plan: to enjoy every single moment of the coming days and years!

At almost midnight, he was walking with his friends, talking and laughing, until suddenly he saw her. He still remembered her face, her eyes, her inviting smile. He found himself walking to her and extending his hand. She was a palmist. She took his hand between her hands and looked to his eyes before she started reading the lines on his palm.

Her body shook, and her smile faded away. She stared in his eyes again, but this time she looked different. She looked scared!

The palmist said, "I see you fall."

With a nervous smile on his face, he said, "What do you mean by fall? Fall in love?"

The palmist said, "My son, before you turn forty years old, you will fall down and meet your death."

Nervous and scared, he snatched back his hand and walked away with his friends without looking back.

The next morning, he woke up exhausted after a night full of nightmares of falling down and dying. He tried to forget last night and focus on his day, but he couldn't stop thinking about the way she'd looked at him, or her prophecy. He decided to cancel all his appointments that day and go see the palmist again. By midday he went back to the same place, but she was not there yet. He couldn't focus on anything else, so he decided to wait for her.

By sunset, he saw her coming with slow, steady steps, a sharp eye, and the same inviting smile. He felt goose bumps because he felt he was looking to his death!

With slow, hesitating steps, he walked to her and gave her his hand.

She looked to him piteously and said, "My son, reading your palm again will not change your fate. What will happen, will happen."

Every day for eighteen years, he repeated that sentence day and night: "What will happen, will happen."

For eighteen years, he had dreams every night about falling and dying.

For eighteen years, this prophecy controlled his life and everything he did. Or to be more specific, this prophecy controlled everything he did *not* do.

His thoughts kept going to this beautiful girl and how their eyes had converged. He'd wanted to talk to her, but he could not because she had taken the elevator, and he had not. He'd stopped using elevators that night because he was scared to fall. He was scared to die.

He remembered the day he'd refused his dream job because it was located in a skyscraper, and he was scared to fall.

He remembered when his parents had had an accident, and rather than flying, he'd driven. But it was too late to say goodbye.

He was scared to fall, and he was scared to die.

And now, after eighteen years, he'd lost everyone— all his friends, all his family. After eighteen years, he'd become alone.

But not anymore. It was five minutes to midnight. Five more minutes, and the prophecy would fail. Five minutes, and he would call all his friends and family. He would explain it to them, and they would forgive him.

His parents would also forgive him. He was sure they'd understand his reasons. They must be watching him from the sky and counting the seconds until they were with him.

Five minutes, and he would be alive!

Here he was, lying on his back and looking to the clear sky and the bright stars—from the bottom of a deep hole where he'd fallen down while he was engrossed in his memories.

He was smiling sarcastically while he muttered, "What will happen, will happen."

But even with the pain all over his body, he still could move his hands and reach to his phone to call for help. Fighting the pain, he pushed himself super hard, held his phone, and started dialing: 9 … 1 … Then he stopped, looked at the phone, and threw it away!

I am not scared to die. I was never scared to die. I was scared to live! The only thing that will give meaning to my meaningless life is to die tonight. But I am not going to die tonight. I already died … eighteen years ago.

His smile faded away. It was midnight, and the stars were so bright.

You may say, "Wait a minute. Something is missing in this story."

What is missing?

"How did he end up in this hole? Is it a construction zone, or a desert, or a sewer hole, or what?"

What else is missing?

"Did the palmist really know the future, or was that just a prank from his friends?"

What else?

"Did he die at the end, or did he survive?"

I have one answer to all these questions: *It does not matter.*

It doesn't matter whether the palmist knew about the future or whether it was a prank. It doesn't matter how and where he fell down in the hole. It doesn't matter whether someone will save him or whether he will die. It doesn't matter whether the prophecy was true or false. What really matters is that he believed the prophecy. What really matters is that he decided to stop enjoying his life until the prophecy either failed or became true.

The real question we need to ask ourselves is, "If your fate is really written on your palm, is it a path you will have to follow, or is it just a forecasting and can be changed?"

You will never know until you know your fate. Maybe your fate is to change your fate.

No matter how your life goes, you will never live it until you enjoy it, until you take risks and are willing to accept the results—not just accepting it but also enjoying it!

We can talk about many stories, whether real or fictional, focusing on the importance of enjoying what you are doing. This is one of the things we all agree about, and we all can give lectures about how it is important to enjoy your life and everything you are doing or trying to achieve on this journey!

So what is stopping us from enjoying our lives? Why are we not enjoying every moment, every victory, and every failure? Why are we missing the old days, looking back to these moments in our lives and saying, "Those were the good days"? Why are we remembering one of our failures in the past, and we're proudly talking about it, how we overcame this failure, and how we enjoyed this experience—yet if we face any failure now, we will not enjoy it that much? Why do we enjoy a moment from the past but not the same moment in present?

I am sure if you repeat these questions to yourself, you will find the answer.

We don't worry about the past, and that is the key to enjoying every moment and every experience you are going through. The key is to control your anxiety. Anxiety is the ingredient that will ruin any enjoyment in your life.

To make sure this point is clear, let us talk about a story that happened to me. My wife and I had our first boy, and then two years later we had our twin boys. I was always worried—worried about their future, worried about their education, worried about their health. Then when I looked back to photos or captured videos, I found enjoyment and blessing—until one time I was checking a video for the kids from few years ago. There was a moment focusing on my face, and I was not happy. I tried to recall any incident that happened on that day that could make me unhappy, but there wasn't any. That was my moment to realize that my anxiety was ruining my enjoyment!

I wouldn't say that was a moment the truth revealed, because I always knew I worried too much, and my wife told me many times that I was not enjoying my time. But in that moment, I realized I needed to change. I needed to focus on the difference between responsibility and anxiety. I had to learn how to take care of my family but also enjoy them as much as I could!

Did I completely change? No. But I am working on it. I shared these thoughts with my wife, adding that she was right about my anxiety. We now remind each other whenever we feel that one of us is starting to ruin the enjoyment of the family journey by worrying too much.

Is it working? Yes, and it feels great.

Do you know what else helped me enjoy my time and this beautiful journey of life? Writing this book, knowing that now I am talking to you! That is why I thank you for giving me this happiness, and that is why I encourage you to do what you enjoy. That is why you should stay honest with yourself. If your passion is acting, then go for it. If it is in writing or drawing, then go for it. No matter your age or your responsibilities, you owe yourself to pursue your dream and do what you enjoy!

Troubleshooting the problem is 50 percent of the solution, but the other 50 percent involves the first eight points on our CHEKMATE strategy. That is why at the beginning of this point, I told you "Enjoy" is the last point but also the core of all the previous points.

- Cry when you feel stressed to release negative feelings, so you can enjoy the journey!
- Stay healthy not just with food but with people in your life, so you can enjoy the journey!
- Learn and educate yourself to have different tools, so you can enjoy your journey!
- Communicate mainly with yourself, so you can enjoy the journey!
- Be a kid, so you can enjoy the journey!
- Meditate to control anxiety, so you can enjoy the journey!
- Accept others and accept failures, so you can enjoy the journey!
- Be tactful, so you can enjoy the journey!

Enjoy every moment, because you deserve to be happy!

Now, my friend, just like everything has an end, our journey in this book is ending here. But remember that every end is a new beginning. Let this be the beginning of a very successful life where you will enjoy every battle and finish it by CHECKMATE.

Live a life fulfilled with this quote:

> The day you born, you were crying, and everyone else was smiling. Live your life so that the day you go, everyone else will be crying, and you will be smiling!

About the Author

WESSAM ELDEIN, OR Sam, as he likes to be called, was born in 1975 in Egypt, Cairo. He got his bachelor's degree in biomedical engineering from Cairo University's Faculty of Engineering Department in 1997.

Sam moved to California in 2008, the same year he got married to his wife, Shaden Nasr. They have three boys, one ten years old and twins eight years old.

Sam got his master's degree in organization leadership from Ashford University in 2010.

Sam has written stories since he was a kid. He always had a dream to publish a book that would explain his thoughts and ideas about how to live a happy life.

Growing up speaking two languages (English and Arabic) helped Sam explore two different cultures and belief systems. You will see that clearly in the examples and stories he uses throughout his book.

Sam believes in interactive reading, and that is why he invites you to reach out to him and share your thoughts about this book via e-mail: checkmatesam@outlook.com.

This book will be a fun learning experiment for both the author and the reader. Sam will be the reader of your thoughts, and you will be the inspiration of his next book.

Then you will be a part of his life, and he will be a part of yours!

Printed in the United States
By Bookmasters